AMC
Field Guide to the
NEW
ENGLAND
ALPINE
SUMMITS

by Nancy G. Slack
& Allison W. Bell

Appalachian Mountain Club Books
Boston, Massachusetts

Cover photograph:
Alpine azaleas blooming in the Alpine Garden on Mt. Washington.
All photographs by Allison W. Bell © 1995 unless otherwise indicated.
© 1995 by Nancy G. Slack and Allison W. Bell. All rights reserved.
Distributed by The Globe Pequot Press, Inc.,
Old Saybrook, Connecticut.

Published by the Appalachian Mountain Club.
No part of this publication may be reproduced or transmitted in any form
or by any means, electronic or mechanical, including photocopying and recording,
or by any information storage or retrieval system, except as may be expressly
permitted by the 1976 Copyright Act or in writing from the
Publisher. Requests for permission should be addressed
in writing to Appalachian Mountain Club Books,
5 Joy Street, Boston, MA 02108.

Library of Congress Cataloging-in-Publication Data
Slack, Nancy G.
Field guide to the New England alpine summits / by Nancy G. Slack;
with photographs by Allison W. Bell.
p.   cm.
ISBN 1-878239-38-4 (alk. paper)
1. Natural history—New England. 2. Mountain plants—New England—
identification. 3. Mountain fauna—New England—identification. I. Title
QH104.5.N4S58 1995
508.74—dc20   95-7306
CIP

The paper used in this publication meets the minimum requirements of
the American National Standard for Information Sciences—Permanence of Paper
for Printed Library Materials, ANSI Z39.48–1984.∞

Due to changes in conditions,
use of the information in this book is at the sole risk of the user.

Design by Allison W. Bell.
Type set in Bembo, Univers, and Snell.
Printed on recycled paper. Printed in the United States of America.
10 9 8 7 6 5 4 3 2 1   95 96 97 98 99

$\mathscr{C}$ONTENTS

"Welcome to the Alpine Zone. Enjoy the fragile beauty.
Be a caring steward. Stay on the trail or walk on bare rocks.
Camp only below timberline. Cook on a stove.
Help preserve the delicate balance of the Alpine Zone.
It's a tough place to grow."
AMC Hut sign

I climbed to my first alpine summit as a young graduate student one June when all the alpine flowers were in bloom. Ever since I have been hooked on both mountain climbing and on this enchanting world above timberline, which I have studied in the Northeast and visited elsewhere in North America and Europe. The New England mountains have some of the most interesting and beautiful alpine vegetation in America, as well as birds, insects, and other animals that make this special world their home.

In New Hampshire, this world exists in its greatest diversity and exuberance on Mt. Washington and the other peaks of the Presidential Range and on Mts. Lafayette and Lincoln on Franconia Ridge. Elsewhere in New England, the alpine areas are smaller and more scattered. The most important are Mt. Mansfield and Camel's Hump in the Green Mountains of Vermont and Katahdin in northern Maine. In addition, many species found on these higher summits can be found on the lower ones, too, even on those that barely reach 4,000 feet. To hike through all the lower mountain zones and finally arrive at the summit is the most satisfying way to view the alpine zone, but this is not the only way. You can drive up Mt. Mansfield, drive or take the cog railway up Mt. Washington. Best of all, you can actually stay in or near the alpine zone yourself at AMC huts, which provide both food and lodging.

The native alpine plants and animals, as well as human visitors, exist in a unique environment. Mt. Washington has some of the most extreme weather in the country, even in the summer. We non-natives must come prepared for this changeable, sometimes dangerous environment. Yet the alpine zone is fragile, too. Boots of unwary hikers can trample rare and endangered native plants. In this book you will get to know the plants and animals that live in this zone and understand something of their lives in their alpine surroundings. It is my hope that you will care about them and their preservation.

For more than thirty years, the *AMC Field Guide to Mountain Flowers of New England* has served well to introduce climbers and other visitors to the alpine flora. The AMC felt an updated, more ecologically oriented guide was needed, one with more color photographs not only of flowers but of birds and other mountain dwellers. We have provided one. Take it in your backpack, and go out and meet the natives. ❧ *Nancy G. Slack*

June in the Alpine Garden on Mt. Washington

This book will take you, in pictures and print, up the highest mountain ranges in New Hampshire, Maine, and Vermont. We will climb to 6,288 feet on Mt. Washington and to over 5,000 feet on its neighboring peaks in the Presidential Range. We'll travel nearly as high on Franconia Ridge and to 5,267 feet on Katahdin in Maine. Mt. Mansfield is only 4,393 feet above sea level, but it has a very extensive alpine ridge. Alpine flora is also found on several peaks over 4,000 feet in all three states. We will start at the trailheads and climb through several forest zones to treeline and above. Although each of these zones has its own diverse and fascinating ecology, our main focus is on life on the summits. In order to understand something of the varied mountain landscape you see, you need to know something of how it came to be—its geological history. In order to survive up there, you need some knowledge of the weather, especially the famous (infamous?) weather of Mt. Washington. But first, a bit of history.

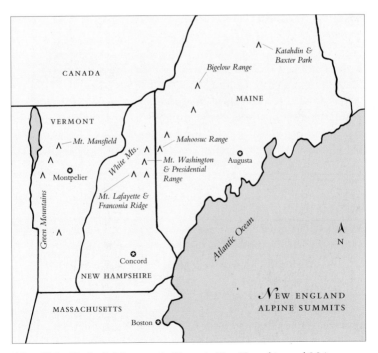

Map of New England alpine areas in Vermont, New Hampshire, and Maine

Mt. Washington summit on a rare warm, sunny day

History of Exploration

The first recorded ascent into New England's alpine zones was in 1642, when the English settler, Darby Field, and two Indian companions climbed Mt. Washington after a long trip up the Saco River from the coast. In 1772, Ira Allen, younger brother of Ethan Allen, climbed Mt. Mansfield and ran a survey line across the crest of the ridge. At that time, that part of Vermont was still uninhabited and Katahdin had hardly been heard of. It was not until 1804 that the first successful climb of Katahdin was made by surveyor Charles Turner. To climb these wilderness peaks before there were trails was an awesome feat.

By the 1820s, the White Mountains had been well explored and had even become a tourist center and a haven for botanists. In 1784, Manasseh Cutler made an expedition with about a dozen others of varied scientific interests and took the first physical measurements on Mt. Washington. Not all made it to the top, which they estimated was at 10,000 feet. Those who did make it got lost on the way down and spent the night huddled around a fire. Cutler made a second expedition in 1804 that included astronomer Nathaniel Bowditch and botanist William D. Peck, for whom the striking yellow mountain avens, *Geum peckii,* is named. This group made and published observations on the alpine plants.

Summit of Mt. Mansfield in Vermont's Green Mountains

In 1811, Alden Partridge climbed Mt. Washington by a route that would later become the Crawford Path. Partridge was an indefatigable hiker who eventually measured the heights of many of the White Mountain and other New England summits. At almost the same time, mineralogist Colonel George Gibbs cut the first path, Gibbs Path, from the east, probably through Tuckerman Ravine. Most early climbers, including botanists, used this route. In 1819, Abel and Ethan Allen Crawford cut an eight-and-a-quarter-mile trail to the summit. Today the Crawford Path is the oldest continuously used hiking trail in the Northeast. A journey along its route will reveal a great many alpine flowers and other features that are shown in this book. In 1821, a second path was built to the base of Ammonoosuc Ravine and then due east up the spur to the summit. By the 1840s, these narrow trails were widened into bridle paths, and many tourists, both men and women, ascended the mountain on horseback.

When the Crawfords began to take visitors up Mt. Washington in the 1820s, most stuck to the trails. But, as Lucy Crawford wrote, "one class of visitors began to wander off trail, and indeed into every nook and cranny of the range." These were early botanists, and there were probably more of them exploring the White Mountains in the twenty years following 1825 than at any time since. Today, many of their names live on in the landmarks of the

Presidentials: Tuckerman Ravine, Boott Spur, Oakes Gulf, and Bigelow Lawn. Many rare plants are named for them, too. The yellow dwarf cinquefoil, *Potentilla robbinsiana,* was named by William Oakes after botanist James W. Robbins who came in 1829. In turn, Edward Tuckerman, an early expert on lichens, named the lichen *Cetraria oakesiana* after Oakes.

Katahdin's Knife Edge

And then there was Franconia Ridge. By 1826, large parties were hiking up a trail on the west side to Mt. Lafayette, 5,225 feet high and well above treeline. Later, Edward Tuckerman made the first botanical survey of this "Great Haystack" and discovered a new site for the dwarf cinquefoil here. On a later trip he found more rare plants including mountain heath. The ever-exploring William Oakes found *Carex scirpoidea,* mountain sedge, there in 1827. Unfortunately, it has disappeared since. The alpine bistort that Tuckerman first found is now also extirpated from Franconia Ridge. Recently, new sites for some rare plants have been found there. In 1994, probably for the first time in the region, this writer found alpine azalea, a tiny pink-flowered dwarf shrub common on Mt. Washington.

Henry David Thoreau first climbed Mt. Washington in 1839 and noted the alpine plants. He climbed Katahdin in 1846 and wrote about his experience in *The Maine Woods.* You can climb with him to the awe-inspiring summit as he describes the moose, bear dens, and mountain cranberries. Thoreau knew the plants well; he made one of the first plant lists for Katahdin.

By the 1850s botanists traveled by horse up Mts. Washington and Lafayette and many other New England peaks. Summit houses were built during this period on Mts. Washington, Mansfield, and Moosilauke. In 1861, the carriage road (later the toll road) opened on Mt. Washington. When the cog railroad carried its first passengers in 1869, the botanists could ride the train. A late-nineteenth-century entomologist, Annie T. Slosson, described them as flying "from side to side of the train car, looking eagerly out and uttering strange exclamations, such as 'Geum!', 'Ledum!'. . . springing from the train at its brief stops to collect plants to the intense amazement and amusement of the unscientific passengers."

Modern visitors to the alpine zone can still travel the toll roads or the cog railway or may choose ski gondolas and aerial tramways. There are no longer bridle paths or summit houses, but you can hike up and stay in an AMC hut.

Geology

The geological events leading to the formation of the New England mountains that we see today started more than 500 million years ago. Much more recent events, such as the time when even the tops of Mt. Washington, Mt. Mansfield, and Katahdin were covered by glacial ice, have also made dramatic changes in the mountain landscape.

The geology of New England involves plate tectonics, the current geological theory that the earth's outer crust consists of shifting plates that have collided over the millennia to produce volcanoes, earthquakes, new mountain ranges, oceans, and continents.

In New England there were two major mountain-building events, or "orogenies," related to plate tectonics. The first, called the Taconic orogeny, took place 460 million years ago. At that time a volcanic island chain, represented today by the Ammonoosuc formation (found at the base of Mt. Madison), rose from a proto-Atlantic Ocean called Iapetus. The island chain collided with what was then the margin of North America (now the Adirondacks), folding undersea sediments of Iapetus to form the Green Mountains of Vermont.

The second orogeny, called the Acadian, took place approximately 400 million years ago. The ocean Iapetus closed as Europe, Africa, and the Americas collided to form a supercontinent, Pangaea (a name meaning "all lands"). Marine sediments consisting of sands and mud under Iapetus were deeply buried in the earth, where intense heat and pressure metamorphosed them into quartzite and schist, respectively. The metamorphosed rock was folded, then thrust up into tall ranges to become the Appalachian Mountains, including the Presidentials with its Littleton and Rangeley formations. When young, these mountains may have been as high as the present-day Himalayas. Where the underground heat and pressure was particularly intense, micas and quartz separated into discrete black-and-white bands to form gneiss (pronounced "nice"). Some Littleton schists under intense heat "sweated out" their quartz, resulting in the milky, snowy white quartz most noticeable in the "moon rocks" near Star Lake, above Madison Hut in the Presidentials. Schist, gneiss, and quartz are on display throughout the Presidentials: Along the Crawford Path northeast of Lakes of the Clouds, cairns are built of schist topped with bright white quartz chunks. Thus, although New Hampshire is called the "Granite State" because much of its rock is just that, the Presidential Range is not.

During the Jurassic Period, about 200 million years ago, a high point of dinosaur life on earth, Pangaea was splitting apart, forming the current Atlantic Ocean. Volcanoes formed and erupted, spewing igneous rock that forms, for example, the Moat and Ossipee ranges southeast of the Presidentials. Another kind of igneous formation is the intrusive dike, formed when molten rock, or magma, intrudes into a fracture, then cools. Mt. Lafayette above Franconia Notch is such a magma dike.

Igneous rock that remained below the surface cooled into the coarse-grained granite for which New Hampshire is famous. Such a mass of granite, formed deep within the earth and then exposed by erosion and uplift, is called a "pluton." Today the plutons of granite can be seen in the Conway region and in the Crawford Notch and Zealand areas. The Katahdin Range in Baxter State Park in northern Maine is another such pluton. Katahdin itself is overlain by a resistant rock cap, granophyre, much harder than even the coarse granite below.

The tectonic uplifts were accompanied and followed by erosion to sculpt the New England mountains into the forms we see today. Mountain streams running down the steep slopes carved deep V-shaped valleys such as the Ammonoosuc Ravine. As the climate cooled, valley glaciers that formed from snow buildup at the higher elevations became ice and flowed downhill. On Mt. Washington,

Tuckerman Ravine and headwall

valley glaciers in the vicinity of Tuckerman and Huntington ravines carved into the mountain to form "glacial cirques" with towering headwalls. Like Tuckerman and Huntington, most cirques in New England are found on the east and north sides of mountains because the prevailing winds caused great accumulations of winter snow in those areas. On Katahdin's east side are large glacial cirques, with steep 2,300-foot headwalls. Katahdin's Cathedral Ridge and Knife Edge are narrow ridges, or "arêtes," separating two cirque basins.

Then came the Pleistocene glaciers, which began approximately two million years ago. During the Wisconsin period of the Pleistocene, fifty thousand years ago, continental ice sheets covered everything—more than a mile thick over the top of Mt. Washington and all the other peaks. Evidence of their passing can be seen in surface scratches called "glacial striae" and scour marks left on exposed bedrock. These striae indicate the glaciers' thickness and the direction they flowed—northwest to southeast in the Presidentials. Continental glaciers also scooped out long U-shaped valleys such as the Crawford Notch and Zealand Notch, while the epoch's valley glaciers carved out spectacular U-shaped valleys such as the Great Gulf on Mt. Washington's north side.

When the last glacier melted about thirteen thousand years ago it left behind the stones, dirt, and debris it was carrying. In the White Mountains this "glacial till" is a foot or two thick. It is found

The Great Gulf, a U-shaped valley carved by glaciers in the Presidential Range

throughout the region—even on the summit of Mt. Washington. Much of the mountain soil, including coarse sand, clay, and angular stones, is made up of this glacial till.

Other evidence of glacial advance and melt-back can be seen in "roches moutonnées," also called sheepbacks or whalebacks. In the Presidentials, Mt. Monroe is a giant roche moutonnée—smooth on the northwest slope, where glaciers wore it down, and jagged on the southeast, where the glaciers' advance tore off chunks of rock. Other glacial formations, called "tarns," are small basins scooped out by the ice. The Lakes of the Clouds are tarns.

Huge boulders, called "glacial erratics," are yet another example of glacial

Glacial erratic stranded above treeline

Soil stripes on Bigelow Lawn on Mt. Washington

landscaping. Erratics were carried off by the glaciers, then deposited "downstream" as the glaciers melted. Sometimes the boulders were carried great distances and thus differ from the local bedrock. Glacial erratics are found throughout New England. Sometimes they are found high up on Katahdin and other peaks. The renowned Glen Boulder on Mt. Washington is a glacial erratic; it was transported from the Randolph area northwest of the mountain to its present location.

Alternate freezing and thawing loosened rock at the joints, resulting in formations such as the Old Man of the Mountain and "felsenmeer," literally a sea of large jagged rock. Trails across felsenmeer slopes can be difficult to negotiate with a big pack,

Felsenmeer on the Crawford Path

Terraces and ground patterns in the Alpine Garden

especially in a high wind.

Freezing and thawing of rocks and movement of soil, a process called solifluction, formed a variety of patterned ground features. Stone circles or polygons, rock stripes, and terraces resulted from differential movement of coarse and fine material. Most of these are "fossil" rock patterns formed in the severe postglacial climate, but similar phenomena still occur today in areas of considerable frost action. Soil stripes, a natural phenomenon, not a human construction, occur on the Bigelow Lawn. Solifluction creates unique microhabitats especially suited to particular alpine plants such as the dwarf cinquefoil.

By thirteen thousand years ago the glaciers had largely melted away and southern New England was free of ice. There were no trees. The landscape looked like the Arctic tundra. Eventually spruces and firs invaded, pushing alpine plants northward and up the mountains. Alpine vegetation remains now only above 4,500 feet and somewhat lower in exposed windswept sites. Nevertheless, there have been alpine plant communities on these sites for ten thousand years. The spruce and fir forests below have almost all been lumbered; even what we call "old-growth" forest is less than two hundred years old. Thus the alpine summits are living museums, truly old communities—to be explored, enjoyed, and protected.

Warning sign on Mt. Washington: "Turn back now if the weather is bad."

Rime ice formations on a rock cairn

Weather & Climate

Seventeenth-century visitors called the northern Presidentials "daunting terrible" and their forests "a vast and howling wilderness." Today the weather is just as severe and unpredictable. Since 1865, when a young climber named Lizzie Bourne fell victim to a storm, more than 110 hikers have perished on Mt. Washington alone. Mt. Washington continues to be the number one killer in the northeastern mountains. What is it about this mountain's weather and climate that can make it so dangerous for the unwary?

First, there are the hurricane-force winds. Wind speed is recorded at over 100 MPH every month of the year. The strongest surface wind ever recorded anywhere on earth, 231 MPH, was clocked here in 1934. Hurricane winds of over 75 MPH occur on half of all winter days and two to four days each summer month.

And then there is the temperature. The average

July temperature is 48° F; the January mean is 6° F. Very often the temperature on top of Mt. Washington is 30 or more degrees colder than at its base. This is because air masses rise when they hit the mountain barrier. With decreased atmospheric pressure at higher elevations, the air expands and cools. An average 3° F temperature drop occurs with every 1,000-foot increase in elevation. In any summer month you can start up Mt. Washington, comfortable

Winter on Mt. Washington

in shorts and a T-shirt, and find yourself in subfreezing conditions above treeline. A visit to the alpine flowers in June means being prepared for challenging weather. In December, January, and February, with the average windchill factored in, unprotected exposed skin can freeze in one minute. Winter climbers take note!

If you are going to be above treeline even from July to mid-September when weather is mildest, you need protection from driving rains. A waterproof jacket, rain pants, and warm wool or polypropylene layers are essential. You will need sunscreen and sunglasses as well. Seventy-five percent of the time the summit is under clouds, but you can still get sunburned. Other necessities, even for day hikers, are good hiking boots, food, water, flashlight, trail guide, map, compass, and a small first aid kit.

The climate on Mt. Washington always has the potential to be "daunting terrible"; the weather is above all changeable. One day in late August, we were on the summit in fog and sleeting rain, in wind so strong we could barely stand. The following day the sky was blue, the wind was down, and the sun was warm enough for sunbathing and butterfly watching. The alpine flowers and birds take all these changes much better than we humans do. Caution is needed in New England's other alpine areas as well, particularly on Katahdin's Knife Edge trail in bad weather.

Northern Hardwood Forest & Transition Zones

To get to the alpine zones of New England, you will travel through several other mountain environments: northern hardwood forest, spruce-fir forest, and a balsam fir zone as you approach treeline. You can begin your climb at many points for the ascent of the Presidentials, Franconia Ridge, Mt. Mansfield, or Katahdin. This account concentrates on the Mt. Washington routes, but trailheads are similar elsewhere. You might begin, for example, at around 1,300 feet on the Appalachian Trail (Webster Cliff Trail) at Route 302 in Crawford Notch. At this elevation, you find yourself in the northern hardwood forest. This is a largely deciduous forest, blazing with color in late September and early October, and dominated by sugar maple, American beech with smooth gray bark, and yellow birch with peeling bark gleaming like brass candlesticks in the autumn sun. Other trees live here, too, including red maple, black cherry, red oak, aspen, paper birch, hemlock, and white pine, as well as a great variety of shrubs, ferns, and wildflowers.

Northern hardwood forest in autumn

Wild sarsaparilla is common in the northern hardwood forest, as is red trillium. Striking painted trillium, white with magenta streaks, and the double-decker Indian cucumber-root are characteristic spring flowers. So are many species of violets, flowering in white, blue, and even yellow. Watch for pink lady-slipper orchids blooming in June with pleated oval leaves. Look, photograph, but do not pick. Hobblebush is a conspicuous shrub, with large, almost heart-shaped leaves and bright red berries in late summer. Like a number of plants and animals of the northern hardwood forest zone, it may also be found higher up into the transition forest zone. Some species are able to survive into the spruce-fir forest zone, and a versatile few, such as Canada mayflower, bluebead lily, and starflower, appear all the way up into sheltered habitats in the alpine zone.

Sugar maple, *Acer saccharum*

American beech, *Fagus grandifolia*

Yellow birch, *Betula alleghaniensis*

The northern hardwood forest is home to a rich diversity of animals. The best times to spot birds and mammals are early and late in the day. Chipmunks, raccoons, white-footed mice, white-tailed deer, and porcupines breed here. Look for bears and moose, which are often seen on Katahdin. Listen for bird songs as you climb, especially in late spring. Red-eyed vireos are the most common bird of this forest, whistling out their "here I am, where are you" songs from the treetops. Hermit thrushes sing haunting woodland flute solos. Ground-nesting ovenbirds are more often heard than

Eastern hemlock, *Tsuga canadensis*

Hobblebush, *Viburnum alnifolium*

seen as they let loose their emphatic "teacher, teacher, teacher" outbursts. Scarlet tanagers and many colorful warblers contrast with the greens of the forest. (You can get a free *White Mountains Bird List* at the Pinkham Notch Visitor Center.)

Amphibians still abound in New England forests, though some species have undergone drastic declines worldwide in recent years. The red-backed salamander is dark with a reddish mid-stripe, or all dark in the "lead-backed" form of the species. The red eft, land form of the aquatic red-spotted newt, is bright orange, a form of warning coloration since it tastes bad to predators. After a hard rain, red efts are so numerous on the trails you need to take care not to step on any. Also common are American toads, wood frogs with their black masks, and tiny spring peepers.

As you ascend the mountain, the landscape changes. At or above 2,000 feet, the northern hardwood forest gives way to a transition forest zone. The Crawford Path, the Ammonoosuc Ravine Trail, and the trails from Pinkham Notch (see *AMC White Mountain Guide or Guide to Mt. Washington and the Presidential Range*) all start in this zone. In the transition forest, spruce and fir trees intermix with sugar maple and other deciduous trees, although in the past, spruce has been heavily logged at lower elevations. Higher up the mountains, spruce becomes the dominant conifer, or cone-bearing tree. As elevation increases, hemlocks and pines drop out as do most of the deciduous trees. Of the major northern hardwood forest trees, yellow birch hangs in there the longest as you climb toward the spruce-fir forest zone.

Spruce-fir forest in Ammonoosuc Ravine

The Spruce-Fir Forest Zone

Many environmental factors change at about 2,500–3,000 feet, and as you climb you notice the forest composition changing around you again. It is not the elevation itself but changing climate that affects the forest. Temperatures are colder here, and thus the growing season is shorter. Precipitation is higher. Soils are wetter, more acid, and less fertile than lower down. Under these conditions, the evergreen conifers, especially red spruce and balsam fir, have an advantage over most deciduous trees. Their needles conserve nutrients and can resume photosynthesis when temperatures are suitable. These two conifers can stand temperatures below -40° F, as can paper birch.

Red spruce and balsam fir are easy to identify: Balsam fir has flat, soft, "friendly" needles with two white "racing stripes" on their undersides. Balsam needles are often bluish green. Red spruce, on the other hand, is usually more yellow green, with prickly needles that are square in cross section rather than flat. Both trees are "Christmas-tree"-shaped, unlike shaggy, lower-elevation hemlocks.

When you arrive in the true spruce-fir zone near 2,700 feet, paper birch is still present, as are striped maple, with green-and-white-striped bark and large "goose-foot" leaves, and mountain maple, with candlelike flower clusters. Mountain ash boasts white

Red spruce, *Picea rubens*

Balsam fir, *Abies balsamea*

Paper birch, *Betula papyrifera*

flowers in spring and bright orange berries in fall. It is a tree indicative of this zone and is often found in open habitats along the trail. Bunchberry, a close relative of the dogwood tree, has four lovely white bracts (leaflike structures that resemble petals) and clusters of red berries later in the season. Other common spruce-fir-zone plants include wood sorrel, with pink-striped white flowers and cloverlike leaves; goldthread, with three shiny evergreen leaflets; twisted stalk, with hanging, bell-shaped flowers; and ghostly white Indian pipes, a true flowering plant that is dependent on tree roots for nourishment. A special flower of the spruce-fir forest is the one that Linnaeus, the eighteenth-century namer of plants and animals, chose for his namesake. *Linnaea borealis,* or twinflower, is a trailing elfin plant with twin tubular pink flowers.

Canada mayflowers, starflowers, and bluebead lilies are still with you as you climb through the spruce-fir zone. As with many flowers that extend through the mountain forest zones, if you find them in bloom at the lower elevations, they may still be in bud as you travel higher. By climbing upward, you are walking back in time; you can enjoy the unique experience of revisiting spring in July at this elevation. In the late summer and fall, tall large-leaved goldenrods and wood asters abound, as do many mushrooms, some of which are poisonous.

The spruce-fir forest has an emerald carpet of ever-green ferns, ground pines, and mosses. Big red-stem moss, *Pleurozium schreberi,* is glossy yellow green, fern-shaped, and easily recognized with its conspicuous reddish stems. Clumps of dark green *Bazzania,* a large leafy liver-wort, luxuriate here. Damp trailside banks are uphol-stered with bright green Sphagnum, or peat moss. Its special water-holding cells retain moisture even in dry weather.

Wood sorrel, *Oxalis acetosella*

Indian pipes, *Monotropa uniflora*

The Balsam Fir Forest Zone

By about 4,000 feet, red spruce also drops out and you continue climbing through almost pure balsam fir forests—the balsam fir zone. The physiology of this tree is adapted to high eleva-tion. It can take the soils here, which are poor because decomposition is slower at lower temperatures and high-er precipitation leaches nutri-ents to lower soil levels.

Many of the same plants found in the spruce-fir zone are present here. So are many of the birds and animals. A number of warblers that migrate south in winter breed in the spruce-fir and

Sharp-leaved aster, *Aster acuminatus*

Twinflower, *Linnaea borealis*

balsam fir zones. Sometimes ten different warbler species can be heard on your hike from the transition zone to the balsam fir forest zone. Their bright colors flash through the forest. "Trees, trees, murmuring trees" sings the black-throated green warbler. Magnolia, blackpoll, and yellow-rumped warblers can be found here and up into the alpine areas. Golden-crowned kinglets call constantly but manage to stay out of sight. Brown-capped boreal chickadees have a different call (a northern accent?) from their black-capped relatives from lower down. Tiny winter wrens wind up for a seemingly impossibly long song, a rapid succession of warbles and trills. Swainson's and Bicknell's thrushes sing their beautiful fluting melodies. Two kinds of yellow-capped woodpeckers are found hammering away in this forest: the black-backed and the rarer three-toed species. Yellow-bellied flycatchers plaintively call "per-wee" or "che-lek." Spruce grouse can be spotted up here, bolder cousins of the shy, lowland ruffed grouse. Red squirrels chatter and scold you—this is their territory, not yours. They are fond of evergreen seeds, as are white-winged and red crossbills, which you may be lucky enough to see. A special treat is to discover a snowshoe hare in its white winter fur or a marten watching you from a tree.

As you continue, you may pass through a solid stand of dead balsam firs—a natural "fir wave." If you look over to other peaks while climbing, you will see this interesting phenomenon from a broader perspective—crescent-shaped bands of dead balsam firs, with declining mature forest on one flank and regenerating fir saplings on the other. The silver gray bands you see in the distance consist of standing trees, "dead on their feet." Fir waves are a natural cyclic disturbance. On wind-exposed slopes, bands of dying trees move through mature fir forests, advancing about three feet per year. Where this phenomenon is well developed, the bands are oriented in numerous rows. The average distance between two waves is about two hundred feet and the repeat time seventy-five years or less. Fir waves can move up or downslope but always in the direction of the prevailing wind.

Fir waves have a significant ecological function. In his book *North Woods,* Peter Marchand considers them an important means of cyclic rejuvenation in the White Mountain subalpine forests, too moist for renewal by fire and too cold for major insect outbreaks. You can see fir waves across Ammonoosuc Ravine from Lakes Hut in good weather. You hike right through them when you climb over Mt. Pierce.

Fir waves on Mt. Madison as seen from the Mt. Washington Auto Road

Landslides and avalanches are also naturally recurring events in this zone. Where the subalpine forest grows on steep slopes, the heavy weight of snow slips and sends an avalanche down the mountain. This happens repeatedly in Huntington and Tuckerman ravines and can be dangerous for spring skiers. Some of these avalanche tracks are bare; others are colonized by resilient mountain alder and other shrubby growth. Landslides, or "slides" to those who like to climb them, are also likely to stay open and visible from afar.

Into the Krummholz

The trees get shorter and the views get longer as you climb into the upper balsam fir zone. Here, the climate becomes about another three degrees colder between 3,000 and 4,000 feet. Fog is more common; precipitation is greater. In the White Mountains, the annual precipitation increases about eight inches for each 1,000 feet of elevation gained. Trees are approaching the upper elevation limit of their upright growth. The balsam fir forest becomes stunted; in some places it must be chopped through for trails. The trees can form a nearly impenetrable thicket, or "tuckamore," the most difficult part of the ascent for bushwhacking early climbers. This is

Landslides and avalanche tracks visible on Mt. Jefferson

probably the largest expanse of never-cut forest in the White Mountains, although there are pockets of beautiful old-growth forest lower down, like those at Gibbs Brook and Nancy Brook.

Beyond the stunted balsam forest is the krummholz ("crooked wood") zone, usually not continuous, composed of dwarfed trees such as balsam fir and black spruce. They often look like bonsai trees, but they have been shaped by natural forces, not human efforts. In the White Mountains and elsewhere in the Northeast, krummholz can be seen in the dwarfed balsam forest ringing the alpine zone and in island patches in favorable sites within the alpine zone itself.

Red spruce does not grow in the krummholz, but a different species, black spruce, does. Black spruce is more blue green than red spruce and is remarkably adaptable. It grows far north in the subarctic, surviving where the permafrost only ever thaws to a foot below the surface. Black spruce is commonly found in lowland bogs but climbs to 5,700 feet on the east, less-wind-exposed side of Mt. Washington. In the alpine zone, it often forms prostrate mats, hugging the ground out of the wind. Its branches form roots when they press against moist ground so that even if its main trunk dies, it has the potential to form a new tree—a reproductive process called layering. Balsam fir also undergoes layering and is the more common of the two trees on the wind-exposed slopes, where clumps of

27

gnarled krummholz extend up to 5,400 feet.

What causes the strange krummholz tree shapes, the dead-branched, flagged, broomsticked, and mopheaded forms? Wind seems to be the main culprit. If you look at a small balsam fir sheltered behind a large rock, you will see that it is straight and treelike until it grows beyond its protector. Then its windward branches die, leaving green branches only on one side—a "flag tree." You may see a whole forest of flag trees, signaling the prevailing wind direction, just below treeline. Strong winds often carry ice particles that kill tree branches in their path by scouring away needles and bark. A tree's leader branches may continually grow and die, forming a gnarled woody survivor, not a "tree-shaped" tree. If the terminal bud does survive, the tree may grow above the zone of ice abrasion and acquire a mopheaded or broomstick shape.

Prostrate balsam fir

Flagged krummholz trees

Broomsticked balsam fir

Treeline signals the beginning of the alpine zone. At treeline, upright trees end and alpine "lawn" begins, interspersed only with occasional krummholz. Every hiker notices this change. We welcome it; we have almost finished our long ascent to the summit. Alpine flowers await us as do, perhaps, magnificent views.

Treeline

Treeline has different causes in different parts of the world. In New England, it has been formed in response to climate, not to human activities such as grazing or woodcutting. There are several climatic factors involved.

Wind is certainly part of the story; as described above, it is hard on upright trees. On cold, wet days it carries water droplets that crystallize onto trees, forming "rime ice." You may admire these one-sided ice sculptures, but they damage trees and reduce their ability to make food through photosynthesis. Low temperatures also play a role in tree-growth limits but do not prevent the growth of at least some trees. Conifers survive temperatures down to -80° F in Alaska and Siberia!

Interestingly, it is not winter cold but the lack of summer heat that correlates best with treeline. The length of the warm growing season determines whether a tree has enough time to produce and harden new growth. If the frosts come too early, new tree shoots will die. A Mt. Washington tree that can stand -50° F in January can have its new shoots damaged at 27° F in a late-August frost. The limit to tree growth in both the alpine zone and in the Arctic is close to the 54° F

Krummholz with rime ice

Patch of krummholz sheltered behind a boulder above treeline

isotherm for the warmest month of the year, usually July in the northern hemisphere. (An isotherm is a line on a map where a particular average temperature occurs.)

Late snow cover can protect trees and be a boon to fast-growing snowbank plants, but it can also effectively shorten the growing season and prevent tree seedlings from getting established.

Those Amazing Alpine Plants

Life in the alpine zone is hard, yet if you reach the Alpine Garden, Monroe Flats, or Bigelow Lawn in the Presidentials, Franconia Ridge, Mt. Mansfield, or Katahdin in mid-June, you will see a dazzling display of flowers and plants that, in its variety and exuberance, seems to defy the extreme conditions.

No one who has witnessed this spring flower show can fail to be impressed by its beauty. For two weeks in June, the slopes are a pastel galaxy, the blossoms beyond counting. Perhaps the most handsome alpine plant is diapensia, which has dark evergreen leaves and waxy white blossoms spangling its compact form. The bearberry willow sports large pink catkins that look too large for its prostrate stems and small leaves. Lapland rosebay explodes with showy magenta flowers, alongside alpine azalea whose starry pink blooms

Diapensia and Lapland rosebay, both true arctic plants

are a delight of color and form. With such an amazing array, spring flower pollinators are kept busy in the alpine gardens.

Wind-pollinated sedges, grasses, and rushes are major components of the alpine flora, although they comprise only a relatively few of the hundreds of species native to the Northeast. *Carex bigelowii,* the sedge named for early botanist Jacob Bigelow, is one of the most successful, covering large areas of moist, exposed meadows. Some of the early grasses and sedges also have lovely flowers— no petals but often colorful stamens, their anthers covered with golden pollen.

Many alpine plants do not have flowers at all. These are spore-bearing plants such as ferns and clubmosses, which have well-developed water- and food-conducting systems. In the snowbank communities these may reach six inches or, in the case of the mountain woodfern, over a foot in height. Other highly successful alpines are mosses and lichens. Mosses and their relatives, the liverworts, flourish on the rocks, in the crannies, and in every rivulet. Lichens come in many colors ranging from gray to bright orange. They adorn every available surface: rocks, windblown ground, branches, and tiny twigs.

Of the great variety of alpines, many are dwarf shrubs, some very dwarf. A good number are related. Lapland rosebay, alpine azalea, several blueberries and bilberries, alpine bearberry, mountain

Dwarf alpine shrubs put on their spring flower display

heath, moss plant, mountain cranberry, and the true small cranberry are all members of the heath family.

How do these alpine plants manage to flourish under extreme conditions? The watchword in the alpine zone is "perennial"—living more than one season. Whether a perennial plant is herbaceous (nonwoody) like mountain sandwort, or woody like alpine azalea, part of the plant survives the winter, storing food for the following seasons. Annual plants, which go through their whole life cycle in one season with only their seeds overwintering, just can't make it above treeline. The growing season is too short.

Herbaceous (nonwoody) Plants in the Alpine Zone

The following abbreviations and symbols are used in this section:

NEW ENGLAND ALPINE DISTRIBUTION

▲W - *found on Mt. Washington*
▲M - *found on Mt. Mansfield*
▲K - *found on Katahdin*

BLOOM TIMES IN THE ALPINE ZONE

❀ MAY - *flowers in May*
❀ JUN - *flowers in June*
❀ JUL - *flowers in July*
❀ AUG - *flowers in August*
❀ SEP - *flowers in September*

Bluebead lily   ▲W,M,K
Clintonia borealis   ❀ JUN–JUL

Found at all mountain elevations up to alpine snowbanks; smooth shiny leaves; blue berries; also called clintonia, named for NY governor Clinton; ≤6" *Lily family*

PLANT HEIGHT IN THE ALPINE ZONE

≤6" - *less than six inches high*
≤12" - *up to twelve inches high*
>12" - *over twelve inches high*

False hellebore or Indian poke   ▲W,M,K
Veratrum viride   ❀ JUL

Common in low-elevation wetlands where it emerges in early spring, also found in alpine streamsides and snowbanks; conspicuously large among other alpine plants; stout stalk; large branched cluster of yellow green flowers; pleated strongly veined leaves; roots and leaves are poisonous; found in North America north to Quebec, south to Georgia; >12" *Lily family*

Canada mayflower ▲W,M,K
Maianthemum canadense ❀ JUN-JUL

Found at all mountain elevations, in protected alpine areas; 2-3 smooth leaves; fragrant flowers; ruby red berries; also called false lily of the valley; ≤6" *Lily family*

Clasping-leaved ▲W,M,K
twisted stalk ❀ JUN-JUL

Streptopus amplexifolius

Found from spruce-fir forests to alpine snowbanks; leaves clasp stem; flowers hang under leaves; oval red berries; ≤12" *Lily family*

Rose twisted stalk ▲W,M,K
Streptopus roseus ❀ JUN-JUL

Found from hardwood forests to alpine snowbanks; nonclasping hairy leaves; pink flowers; oval red berries (hybrid plant has wine red flowers); ≤12" *Lily family*

Tall leafy white orchid ▲W,M,K
Habenaria dilatata ❀ JUL-AUG

In moist areas, from subalpine forests and bogs to alpine ravines and streamsides; narrow leaves along stem; spike of spicy, fragrant spurred flowers; ≤12" *Orchid family*

Mountain sorrel ▲W
Oxyria digyna ✸ JUL

Found in alpine streamsides and ravines; kidney-shaped leaves; green to red flowers; also found in w. U.S. mountains, Eurasia; ≤12" *Buckwheat family*

Alpine bistort ▲W,M,K
Polygonum viviparum ✸ JUL

Found in moist alpine areas; many tiny flowers on long stem; reproduces vegetatively by bulblets; also found in w. U.S., Arctic, and Eurasia; ≤12" *Buckwheat family*

Mountain sandwort ▲W,M,K
Arenaria groenlandica ✸ JUL–SEP

Widely distributed in alpine zone common along trails; a pioneer plant in areas disturbed by frost action, trail erosion, etc.; grows in tufts or cushions sometimes covering large areas; many 5-petaled flowers on stalks; blooms throughout the summer until frost; found in N.A., n. to Greenland, s. to coastal ME; related species are found on w. U.S. mountains; ≤6" *Pink family*

Mountain stitchwort ▲W,M
Stellaria borealis ❀ JUL–SEP
Common in moist alpine areas up
to Mt. Washington summit;
opposite leaves; weak stems; tiny
flowers; also found in w. N.A.
and Arctic; ≤12" *Pink family*

Moss campion ▲W
Silene acaulis ❀ JUN
Dwarf alpine cushion plant; leaves
are like coarse moss; 5-lobed,
tubular showy flowers; tap root;
also found in w. and arctic N.A.,
Eurasia; ≤6" *Pink family*

Goldthread ▲W,M,K
Coptis trifolia ❀ JUN–JUL
Found in all mountain zones; 3
shiny evergreen leaflets; single
flower; bright yellow rhizomes;
found from NC to Labrador, Asia;
≤6" *Buttercup family*

Alpine cress ▲W,K
Cardamine bellidifolia ❀ JUL–AUG
Dwarf plant of alpine ravines;
small oval leaves; 4-part white
flowers; long narrow seedpods;
also found in Arctic, Eurasia; ≤6"
Mustard family

Alpine brook saxifrage ▲W
Saxifraga rivularis ✿ JUL–AUG

Rare in alpine ravines, also found near Lakes Hut and on Mt. Washington summit near Tip Top House; small leaves have 3–7 lobes; tiny 5-part white flowers; plant grows in tufts among boulders; saxifrage means "rock breaker"; Mt. Washington is its southernmost site; also found in Arctic to Ellesmere Island, 82° N, and Eurasia; ≤6" *Saxifrage family*

Star saxifrage ▲K
Saxifraga foliolosa ✿ JUL–AUG

An arctic plant; once fairly common on Katahdin, now rare; basal spatula-shaped leaves; most flowers replaced by leafy tufts; found on mossy rocks; ≤6" *Saxifrage family*

White mountain-saxifrage ▲W,K
Saxifraga aizoon ✿ JUL

Rare alpine plant; easily identified by its lime-encrusted pores; white flower cluster at top of stem; also found at Smuggler's Notch in VT and Arctic; ≤6" *Saxifrage family*

Dwarf cinquefoil ▲W
Potentilla robbinsiana ❀ JUN

Rarest alpine plant in New England, found only on Mt. Washington and the Franconia Range; small leaves have 3 deeply toothed leaflets; flowers are ¼" across with 5 petals; discovered by early botanist and ornithologist Thomas Nuttall; named by William Oakes (Oakes Gulf) for botanist James W. Robbins; federally protected; ≤6" *Rose family*

Three-toothed cinquefoil ▲W,M,K
Potentilla tridentata ❀ JUL–SEP

Found on exposed ledges and rocky alpine habitats; 3-toothed evergreen leaflets turn red in fall; found s. to GA, n. to Greenland and Labrador ; ≤6" *Rose family*

Alpine marsh violet ▲W,K
Viola palustris ❀ JUN–JUL

Found in alpine and subalpine ravines and streamsides; heart-shaped leaves; white to lavender flowers; found n. to Newfoundland, and in w. U.S.; ≤6" *Violet family*

Mountain avens ▲W
Geum peckii ✤ JUN–AUG

Found in alpine and subalpine streamsides, alpine snowbanks, and bogs;
large textured leaves turn crimson in fall; showy flowers on long stems;
named for early botanist William Peck; found only in White Mountains
and Nova Scotia; *Geum rivale,* purple avens, is found in alpine ravines; ≤12"
Rose family

Fireweed ▲W,M,K
Epilobium angustifolium ✤ JUL–AUG

Common lowland plant occasionally found above treeline; loose
stalk of 4-petaled flowers; subarctic, found s. to NC mountains;
>12" *Evening primrose family*

Alpine willow-herb ▲W,K
Epilobium hornemanii ✤ JUN–AUG

Found in alpine streamsides and
ravines; opposite toothed leaves;
pink flowers; long seedpods; found
in arctic N.A. and Eurasia; ≤12"
Evening primrose family

Bunchberry or dwarf cornel
Cornus canadensis

▲W,M,K
✿ JUN–JUL

Found at all mountain elevations from hardwood forest into krummholz and alpine areas; whorl of 4-6 leaves that are darker color above treeline; 4 white petallike bracts; inconspicuous greenish central flowers become bright scarlet bunch of berries in late summer; found across North America from NM to WV and Greenland to Alaska, Asia; ≤6" *Dogwood family*

Starflower
Trientalis borealis

▲W,M,K
✿ JUL–AUG

Found at all mountain elevations; plants can be tiny in alpine zone; flowers have 7 petals; borealis means "of the north"; found n. to Labrador; ≤6" *Primrose family*

Alpine speedwell
Veronica wormskjoldii

▲W,K
✿ JUL–AUG

Found in alpine ravines; stems and opposite leaves are hairy; blue flowers have 4 petals, 2 stamens; also found in w. N.A., Greenland to Alaska; ≤12" *Figwort family*

Pale painted cup ▲W,K
Castilleja septentrionalis ❀ JUL–AUG
Found in moist alpine areas; tall
leafy spike; semiparasitic; related
to western Indian paintbrushes;
found north to Labrador; >12"
Figwort family

Eyebright ▲W,K
Euphrasia oakesii ❀ JUL–AUG
Found in alpine zone only; small
plant with round toothed leaves;
semiparasitic; tiny burgundy or
white flowers; found north to
Labrador; ≤6" *Figwort family*

Alpine bluet ▲W
Hedyotis caerulea ❀ JUN–JUL
This white-flowered variety of the blue-flowered lowland species is found
in alpine snowbanks and moist places above treeline; tiny opposite leaves;
honey-scented 4-part flowers have yellow centers; found only in White
Mountains and on the islands of St. Pierre and Miquelon near Newfoundland; common bluet is sometimes found above treeline; ≤6" *Madder family*

Harebell or bluebell
▲W,M,K
Campanula rotundifolia
❀ JUL–SEP

Found at lower elevations and in alpine zone where it is one of the loveli-
est summer flowers; only the leaves at base of the plant are round or
rotund, stem leaves are narrow; delicate stems support nodding bell-shaped
flowers, usually a single blossom in the alpine zone; found north to
Newfoundland, western North America, Alps, Asia; ≤12" *Bluebell family*

Alpine goldenrod
▲W,M,K
Solidago cutleri
❀ JUL–SEP

The most common and smallest goldenrod in alpine zone, grows only
above treeline; 2-7 leaves on stem; named for eighteenth-century botanist
Manasseh Cutler; found on mountains from ME to NY; *Solidago simplex
var. monticola,* Rand's goldenrod, is taller with more leaves and is occasional
in alpine zone; the two species hybridize; ≤12" *Composite family*

Large-leaved goldenrod ▲W,M,K
Solidago macrophylla ❀ JUL–SEP

Found in all mountain zones to alpine snowbanks; large broad leaves; ½ " flower heads; found from Labrador s. to NY and Mt. Greylock; >12" *Composite family*

Mountain aster ▲W,M,K
Aster crenifolius ❀ AUG–SEP

Found in moist alpine and subalpine areas; hairy stems and leaves; flowers heads surrounded by leafy bracts; found north to Labrador; >12" *Composite family*

Arnica ▲W,K
Arnica lanceolata ❀ JUL–SEP

Found in alpine ravines and on ravine headwalls; leaves and stems are hairy; leaves are variable; many 2" flower heads; found in North America north to Gaspé, west to Colorado, California, Alberta, and British Columbia; several other yellow-flowered arnica species are found in Rocky Mountains; >12" *Composite family*

Boott's rattlesnake-root ▲W,M,K
Prenanthes boottii ✿ JUL–SEP

Strictly an alpine plant; triangular or heart-shaped leaves; named for its discoverer J. W. Boott; found only on New England and NY summits; ≤12" *Composite family*

Low rattlesnake-root ▲W,K
Prenanthes trifoliolata ✿ JUL–SEP

Found at all mountain elevations, alpine variety is shorter; variable 3-part leaves; the dwarf variety is found from Labrador to NY mountains; ≤12" *Composite family*

Orange hawkweed ▲W,M,K
Hieracium aurantiacum ✿ JUL–SEP

Found at all mountain elevations, into alpine zone; a non-native weed introduced from Europe; found n. to Nova Scotia, s. to NC; ≤12" *Composite family*

Yarrow ▲W,M,K
Achillea millefolium ✿ JUL–SEP

Found at all mountain elevations, into alpine zone; featherlike leaves; a non-native weed introduced from Europe; also found across N.A.; ≤12" *Composite family*

Balsam fir ▲W,M,K
Abies balsamea

Found from transition into alpine zone as dwarf tree and mat former; erect cones; flat needles with white stripes below; found from Labrador to VA; >12" *Pine family*

Trees & Shrubs
in the Alpine Zone

The following abbreviations and symbols are used in this section:

NEW ENGLAND ALPINE DISTRIBUTION
▲W - *found on Mt. Washington*
▲M - *found on Mt. Mansfield*
▲K - *found on Katahdin*

BLOOM TIMES IN THE ALPINE ZONE
❀ MAY - *flowers in May*
❀ JUN - *flowers in June*
❀ JUL - *flowers in July*
❀ AUG - *flowers in August*

PLANT HEIGHT IN THE ALPINE ZONE
≤6" - *less than six inches high*
≤12" - *up to twelve inches high*
>12" - *over twelve inches high*

Black spruce ▲W,M,K
Picea mariana

Found in krummholz and prostrate mats in the alpine zone, also in lowland bogs; prickly needles; also found from Labrador and Alaska s. to WV; >12" *Pine family*

Dwarf willow ▲W,K
Salix herbacea ❀ JUL–AUG

Found in alpine zone only; tiny trailing shrub; round leaves; flowers in short catkins; extirpated in Adirondacks; also found in Arctic, Greenland, Asia; ≤6" *Willow family*

Bearberry willow ▲W,M,K
Salix uva-ursi ❀ JUN

Found in alpine zone only; matted prostrate shrub, much more common than dwarf willow; small, oval toothed leaves are green and veined above, pale beneath; flowers in large pinkish catkins; fertilized flowers form smooth brown capsules; named for resemblance of leaves to bearberry; also found in arctic North America north to Greenland; ≤6" *Willow family*

Arctic-loving willow ▲K
Salix arctophila

Found in alpine zone only; dwarf prostrate shrub; bluntly pointed, shiny, nontoothed leaves; flowers in catkins; rare on Katahdin; also found in Arctic; ≤6" *Willow family*

Silver willow ▲W,K
Salix argyrocarpa ❀ JUN–JUL

Found in alpine ravines and moist areas; upright shrub; green leaves, impressed veins, silvery hairs beneath; silky capsules; also found n. to Labrador; >12" *Willow family*

Tea-leaved willow ▲W,M,K
Salix planifolia ❀ JUN-JUL
Found in moist alpine areas, subalpine forests on Mt. Mansfield;
upright shrub; leaves whitish
below; found n. to Labrador and
Alberta; >12" *Willow family*

Heart-leaved paper birch ▲W,M,K
Betula papyrifera var.
cordifolia ❀ MAY-JUN
Found in upper elevations, to
alpine zone; heart-shaped leaves;
reddish bark; found n. to Labrador; >12" *Birch family*

Dwarf birch ▲W,K
Betula glandulosa ❀ JUN-JUL
Found in alpine zone only; low shrub, varies in height from prostrate to 2
feet tall; small rounded leaves with scalloped edges; in fall leaves turn a
handsome deep red; catkins to an inch long; found north to Labrador, Asia;
Betula x minor, mountain birch, is a hybrid species with larger pointed
leaves; ≤12" *Birch family*

Mountain alder ▲W,M,K
Alnus viridis ❀ JUN

Found along streams in subalpine forests, alpine ravines; dwarf shrub in alpine zone; finely toothed leaves; found in Arctic n. to Labrador, Alaska; >12" *Birch family*

Skunk currant ▲W,K
Ribes glandulosum ❀ MAY–JUN

Found at all elevations to alpine zone; low shrub; smooth stems; crushed leaves have skunklike odor; red bristly berries; found n. to Labrador; >12" *Gooseberry family*

Northern meadowsweet ▲W,M,K
Spiraea latifolia ❀ JUL–SEP

Shrub found at all mountain elevations; alpine variety in alpine ravines and meadows has short compact flower heads; found s. to VA, n. to Labrador; >12" *Rose family*

Mountain ash ▲W,M,K
Sorbus decora ❀ JUN–JUL

Tree found in transition zone to alpine zone; compound leaves; white flower clusters; close relative *S. americana* blooms first; found n. to Greenland; >12" *Rose family*

Bartram's shadbush ▲W,M,K
Amelanchier bartramiana ❀ MAY

Found from subalpine forests to alpine zone; finely toothed leaves; named for William Bartram, early plant explorer; found s. to MA, n. to Labrador; >12" *Rose family*

Cloudberry ▲W
Rubus chamaemorus ❀ JUN-JUL

Found in alpine bogs in Presidentials and Mahoosucs; also called baked apple berry; single white flower; found n. to Greenland, Eurasia; ≤12" *Rose family*

Dwarf raspberry ▲W,M,K
Rubus pubescens ❀ JUN-JUL

Found at all elevations, in alpine ravines and meadows; trailing stem without prickles; white flowers; red berries; found n. to Labrador, w. to CO; ≤12" *Rose family*

Black crowberry ▲W,M,K
Empetrum nigrum ❀ MAY-JUN

Found in alpine zone and rocky lower summits; mat-forming shrub; tiny evergreen leaves; black berries; also found in Arctic n. to Greenland; ≤6" *Crowberry family*

Labrador tea ▲W,M,K

Ledum groenlandicum ❀ JUN

Shrub found in bogs and at all elevations into alpine zone; thick evergreen leaves, woolly beneath; found n. to Labrador, Greenland, and Alaska; >12" *Heath family*

Rhodora ▲W,M,K

Rhododendron canadense ❀ MAY-JUN

Shrub found in bogs and up to alpine zone; downy deciduous leaves; flowers bloom before leaves unfold; found from Newfoundland to PA; >12" *Heath family*

Lapland rosebay ▲W,K

Rhododendron lapponicum ❀ MAY-JUN

Found only in alpine zone; low prostrate shrub; magenta-purple flowers up to 1" across seem large for plant's size; evergreen, elliptical leaves with scurfy scales; dry seedpods; flowers at same time as alpine azalea and diapensia; found in Arctic south to Adirondacks and Wisconsin Dells, also Eurasia including Lapland; ≤12" *Heath family*

Alpine azalea ▲W,K
Loiseleuria procumbens ✿ MAY-JUN
Found in alpine zone only; dwarf
mat-forming shrub; ½" evergreen
leaves; small red seedpods; also
found in Arctic to Greenland,
Alaska, Eurasia; ≤6" *Heath family*

Bog laurel or pale laurel ▲W,M,K
Kalmia polifolia ✿ JUN-JUL
Found in low-elevation bogs and
moist alpine areas; green shiny
leaves, white underneath; found s.
to NJ, n. to Labrador, w. to OR,
AK; ≤12" *Heath family*

Mountain heath ▲W,K
Phyllodoce caerulea ✿ JUN
Found only in alpine zone, often
in alpine snowbank communities;
tiny, evergreen needlelike leaves;
also found in Arctic, Eurasia; ≤6"
Heath family

Leatherleaf ▲W,M,K
Chamaedaphne calyculata ✿ MAY-JUN
Shrub found in low-elevation bogs
and in alpine zone; tough, leathery
scaly leaves; several varieties;
found n. to Labrador, Eurasia;
≤12" *Heath family*

Moss plant ▲W,K
Cassiope hypnoides ❀ JUN
Found in alpine snowbank communities; small, pointed evergreen
leaves; hypnoides means "moss-
like"; also found in Arctic, Greenland, Eurasia; ≤6" *Heath family*

Alpine bearberry ▲W,K
Arctostaphylos alpina ❀ JUN
Found only in alpine zone; leaves
are veined and textured, turn deep
red in fall; small white flowers;
berries are rare; also found in
Arctic, Eurasia; ≤6" *Heath family*

Creeping snowberry ▲W,M,K
Gaultheria hispidula ❀ JUN
Found in spruce-fir zone, krummholz, into alpine areas; evergreen
leaves; tiny flowers; white berries;
found n. to Labrador, s. to NC;
≤6" *Heath family*

Bog bilberry ▲W,M,K
Vaccinium uliginosum ❀ JUN
Found in many alpine communities; rounded, toothless, blue
green leaves turn purple in fall;
blue berries; found s. to MI, n. to
Ellesmere Island; ≤12" *Heath family*

Low sweet blueberry ▲W,M,K
Vaccinium angustifolium ❀ JUN

Found from lowlands to alpine
zone; narrow, finely toothed
leaves; found n. to Labrador; *V.
boreale* is very dwarf alpine blueberry species; ≤12" *Heath family*

Small cranberry ▲W,M,K
Vaccinium oxycoccos ❀ JUN-JUL

Found in lowland and alpine bogs;
creeping stems; small leaves;
shooting-star-like flowers; red
berries; found n. to Greenland, s.
to VA, Eurasia; ≤12" *Heath family*

Dwarf bilberry ▲W,M,K
Vaccinium cespitosum ❀ JUN-JUL

Dwarf shrub found in alpine zone
and on lower bare summits;
toothed leaves are broadest above
middle; blue berries; found n. to
Labrador; ≤6" *Heath family*

Mountain cranberry ▲W,M,K
Vaccinium vitis-idaea ❀ JUN

Shrub found in alpine zone and
on lower summits; mat-forming;
red berries; also called lingonberry;
found in Arctic, n. to Greenland,
Europe, e. Asia; ≤6" *Heath family*

Diapensia ▲W,M,K

Diapensia lapponica ✽ MAY–JUN

Found in alpine zone, often in the most extreme wind-exposed sites; forms compact evergreen cushions or mats; narrow spatulate leaves; waxy, white, 5-part flowers on short stalks above plant cushion; one of the earliest plants to bloom above treeline, often with alpine azalea and Lapland rosebay; found in Arctic to 82° N, Eurasia; ≤6" *Diapensia family*

Peter Zika

Mountain fly honeysuckle ▲W,K

Lonicera coerulea ✽ JUN–JUL

Shrub found in moist alpine areas, ravines; blunt leaves; paired flowers; twin berries; var. *villosa* is found n. to Hudson Bay, s. to NH; >12" *Honeysuckle family*

Squashberry ▲W,M,K

Viburnum edule ✽ JUN–JUL

Found at all elevations in moist places; maplelike leaves; flowers in clusters; fruit yellow to red; found n. to Labrador, s. to PA, Asia; >12" *Honeysuckle family*

Fir clubmoss ▲W,M,K
Lycopodium selago
Found in alpine zone and on rocky peaks; small low tufts; spore cases at base of small evergreen leaves

Clubmosses & Ferns in the Alpine Zone

The following abbreviations and symbols are used in this section:

NEW ENGLAND ALPINE DISTRIBUTION

▲W - *found on Mt. Washington*
▲M - *found on Mt. Mansfield*
▲K - *found on Katahdin*

Bristly clubmoss ▲W,M,K
Lycopodium annotinum
Found at all elevations into alpine zone; creeping stem; upright branches with unstalked cones

Groundpine ▲W,M,K
Lycopodium obscurum
Found at all elevations into alpine zone; creeping stem; forked evergreen branches; upright cones

Long beech fern ▲W,M,K
Thelypteris phegopteris
Found at all elevations into alpine zone; variable size; triangular fronds; lower leaflets point down

Mountain woodfern ▲W,M,K
Dryopteris campyloptera
Found at all elevations, alpine snowbank communities; broad fronds with toothy divisions

55

Grasses, Sedges, & Rushes in the Alpine Zone

The following abbreviations and symbols are used in this section:

NEW ENGLAND ALPINE DISTRIBUTION
▲w - *found on Mt. Washington*
▲M - *found on Mt. Mansfield*
▲K - *found on Katahdin*

PLANT HEIGHT IN THE ALPINE ZONE
≤6" - *less than six inches high*
≤12" - *up to twelve inches high*
>12" - *over twelve inches high*

Boreal bentgrass
Agrostis mertensii

Common in alpine zone; small fine grass; grows in tufts; single-flowered spikelets; bent awns; found n. to Greenland, s. to NH, and on Roan Mt., NC; ≤6"

Alpine sweetgrass   ▲W,M,K
Hierochloe alpina

Fragrant grass of the alpine zone; tufted; short leaves; florets with ¼" awns; ≤12"

Alpine timothy   ▲W,K
Phleum alpinum

Found only in alpine zone; short cylindrical flower spike; found n. to Greenland; ≤12"

Spiked trisetum   ▲W,M
Trisetum spicatum

Found in alpine zone; leafy stems; dense, spiky flower heads; curved awns; ≤12"

Crinkled hairgrass ▲W,M,K

Deschampsia flexuosa

Found at all elevations into alpine zone; hair-like leaves; florets have bent awns; ≤12"

Bluejoint ▲W,M,K

Calamagrostis canadensis

Found at lower eleva-tions, alpine ravines, and alpine zone; large, purplish plumelike flower clusters; >12"

Kentucky bluegrass ▲W

Poa pratensis

An attractive tall grass found in alpine zone; alien introduced from Europe; >12"

Mountain sedge ▲W,M,K

Carex scirpoidea

Found in alpine zone; unusual, separate male and female spikes; ≤12"

Bigelow's sedge ▲W,M,K

Carex bigelowii

Forms large alpine meadows; dried-up leaf bases; dark pur-plish spikes; ≤12"

Brownish sedge ▲W,M,K

Carex brunnescens

Found in all zones, frequent in alpine; small flower heads; brown or green; ≤12"

Hairlike sedge ▲W

Carex capillaris

Small delicate tussock sedge; grows in moist alpine areas; few small spikes on thin drooping stems; ≤6"

Deer's-hair sedge ▲W,M,K

Scirpus caespitosus

Important plant in alpine communities; dense tufts; turns tawny in fall; ≤12"

Cotton sedge ▲W,M,K

Eriophorum vaginatum var. spissum

In bogs at all elevations; clump of fluffy hairs on stalk; also called hare's-tail; ≤12"

Three-forked rush or highland rush ▲W,M,K

Juncus trifidus

A major component of alpine turfs; 2-3 leaves at top of stem surround spikes; ≤12"

Small-flowered woodrush ▲W,M,K

Luzula parviflora

Found at all elevations to alpine zone; broad basal leaves; many nodding flowers; ≤12"

Spiked woodrush ▲W,M,K

Luzula spicata

Found in alpine lawns; large, brown, nodding flower spikes; narrow basal leaves; ≤12"

Mosses, Liverworts, & Lichens

Mosses and their relatives the liverworts comprise the bryophytes, a group of nonflowering plants that ranges from the tropics to the Arctic and Antarctic. Mosses can take moisture and nutrients directly through their surface cells. This enables them to begin photosynthesis whenever the temperature is above freezing in any season, which gives them an advantage over rooted plants. Some common temperate species, including several haircap mosses, do extremely well above treeline. Some of their relatives are found only in the alpine zone and perhaps the krummholz, but not farther downslope. These haircap mosses all have thickened, opaque leaves. In addition, several species have protective hair points at the ends of the leaves. Although mosses are officially nonvascular plants, haircap mosses actually have a water-conducting system and can obtain water and nutrients from unfrozen soil. Some mosses look completely dried out and dead when the sun does shine but recover and begin to photosynthesize as soon as there is moisture. A good example is granite moss, *Andreaea,* which forms the small rounded black clumps on alpine rocks.

Mosses grow in a variety of habitats. Many live as hangers-on (epiphytes but not parasites) on living trees in the subalpine forest. In the alpine zone they grow in nearly all of the alpine communities but are most prevalent in the moister ones such as streamsides and bogs. The big red-stem moss, a ground cover in the subalpine forests, finds a home above treeline in snowbank and other sheltered communities, as do other "feather" mosses. Sphagnum, or peat mosses are ubiquitous in moist habitats. A number of New England alpine bog plants grow only in sphagnum moss. Several, though not all, of the alpine streamside and bog peat mosses make anthocyanins and other pigments when exposed to light and are various shades of pink, red, and brown. *Sphagnum girgensohnii* is green, genetically unable to make red pigments. It is the most common trailside plant in wet places below the treeline.

Liverworts are so named because of their supposed resemblance to livers and were once a sought-after cure for liver ailments. Most species do not in the least resemble livers but have stems with leaves. Unlike mosses, the leaves of liverworts are in two ranks so that the stems appear flattened. Even more than mosses, they prefer moist habitats such as streams and wet rock crevices. Most are small and inconspicuous plants, but there are exceptions. Three-lobed bazzania is a giant among leafy liverworts. It is conspicuous in large, dark green clumps in the subalpine fir forest. Another large liverwort, *Ptilidium ciliare,* is a regular inhabitant of the krummholz and alpine heath habitats. It stands upright an inch high. With a hand lens you can see its leaves, divided into ciliate, or hairlike, segments.

Lichens are extraordinary organisms. They are probably the best adapted and certainly the most diverse group in the alpine zone. Lichens are the result of a symbiotic relationship, almost certainly mutually beneficial, between a fungus and a green alga or cyanobacterium. In general, the fungus provides protection to the algal or cyanobacterial cells, and the latter provide photosynthates for the fungus, though that is an oversimplified description of the lichen symbiosis. Most important for our concerns, the lichen is far more durable in the alpine zone than either of its components. Other fungi, such as mushrooms, do live on White Mountain summits, as do stream algae, but lichens are much more dominant and diverse. Like the mosses, they are able to absorb water directly and are adapted for photosynthesis at very low temperatures.

Moreover, lichens produce a great many chemical by-products, including pigments. Lichens add color to the alpine zones in all the New England mountains. They come in photogenic yellow, orange, rust, green, white, gray, black, and various shades of tan and brown. Lichens also produce an array of acids, which aid in breaking down their rock hosts. Lichens inhabit all of the plant communities discussed above: Some of those on Mt. Washington are also found far to the north in subarctic and Arctic Canada. On some New England summits, there are boulder fields where nothing is able to grow except a few moss species and a variety of lichens.

Lichen species come in several growth types: crustose (crustlike) lichens, which grow on rock and tree surfaces; foliose (leaflike) lichens, very common on alpine soils and even on peat mosses in bogs; and upright fruticose (shrubby) lichens. Fruticose lichens include the various "reindeer" lichens, so-called because they are eaten by European reindeer.

There is at present no comprehensive list of either mosses or lichens of the New England alpine summits, but several people including the author of this book are currently working on one for Mt. Washington.

Mosses, Liverworts, & Lichens in the Alpine Zone

Robert Wesley

Big red-stem moss
Pleurozium schreberi

The most common moss of the balsam fir forest; also in protected alpine sites; obvious red stems

Big red peat moss
Sphagnum magellanicum

Found in lowland and alpine bogs; only large turgid peat moss with red pigment; grows worldwide

Green peat moss
Sphagnum girgensohnii

The most common trailside peat moss in all zones to krummholz; star-shaped heads; long branches

Blue green pogonatum
Pogonatum urnigerum

Often found along alpine trails; broad-leaved rosettes; cylindrical nonangled capsules

Bog haircap moss
Polytrichum strictum

Common in alpine zone and lowland bogs; stiff erect plants; gray threads on stem; angled capsules

Granite moss (reddish black)
Andreaea rupestris
Shag moss (yellowish green)
Racomitrium heterostichum
Both grow on rocks in alpine zone

Woolly shag moss
Racomitrium lanuginosum
Forms large hoary clumps or mats in the alpine zone; leaf tips have rough, toothed colorless hair points

Turf broom moss
Dicranum elongatum
This arctic moss forms compact tufts on Mt. Washington; common broom moss is greener

Pincushion grimmia
Grimmia pulvinata
Attractive, small, white-tipped cushions on rocks in alpine zone; ribbed capsules on curved stalks

Turgid bog moss
Aulocomnium turgidum
An arctic moss found on Mt. Washington and Katahdin; overlapping leaves; resembles worms

Three-lobed bazzania
Bazzania trilobata
Large leafy liverwort; forms big clumps in subalpine forest; 3-toothed leaves in 2 ranks

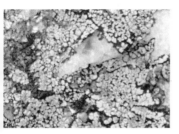

Map lichen
Rhizocarpon geographicum

Very common crust lichen on rocks in the alpine zone; yellow green color; "continent" patterns

Rusty rock lichen
Tremolecia atrata

Common crust lichen in the alpine zone; dull orange red color; grows on exposed on rocks

Target lichen
Arctoparmelia centrifuga

Foliose lichen that grows in concentric rings; recolonizes inner portions as center decays

Red-tipped goblet lichen
Cladonia pleurota

One of several lichens found in the alpine zone with red reproductive structures; cups short and stout

Beaked rock tripe
Umbilicaria proboscidea

Rock tripes attach to rock by central cord, often grow on alpine boulders; eaten by arctic musk ox

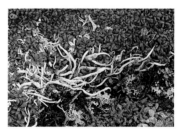

Worm lichen
Thamnolia vermicularis

Hollow, unbranched and wormlike; *T. vermicularis* and *T. subuliformis* look identical but differ chemically

Snow lichen
Cetraria nivalis

Alpine and subalpine areas on Mt. Washington; found in late snow-melt areas in Arctic; flattened lobes

Iceland lichen
Cetraria laevigata

Tan or brown; broad lobes; important component of alpine communities; crisp and brittle when dry

Easter lichen
Stereocaulon sp.

Common in alpine zone; short solid stalks and small leaflike lobes; species are difficult to identify

Reindeer lichen *Cladina rangiferina*
Alpine reindeer lichen *C. stellaris*

Common in alpine zone and other exposed areas; eaten by reindeer; *C. stellaris* is smaller and bushier

Quill lichen
Cladonia amaurocraea

Grows on soil over rocks in the alpine zone and other open areas; shiny, sometimes with cups

"Moss-eater" lichen
Bryophagus gleopcapsa

Grows over moss; crackled surface; gelatinous when wet; recently discovered on Mt. Washington

Adaptations of Alpine Plants

To survive in the alpine environment, plants capitalize on several adaptations. Small size is probably the most common characteristic of alpine plants. It is an advantage in keeping stems and especially buds out of the worst weather. It is also an energy saver: The plant has to make less food to produce its leaves, flowers, fruit, and seeds. Some alpine flowering plants such as moss plant, *Cassiope,* can go through their whole cycle, producing flowers and fruit, while only attaining an inch in height.

Shape is important, too. Cushion-shaped plants have great advantages. Wind can flow over them as over an airplane wing. The dark, tightly packed evergreen leaves of diapensia absorb heat, creating higher temperatures inside a diapensia cushion than in the frigid outside air, enhancing growth. Some cushion plants such as moss campion have central roots that anchor the cushion. These plants often put their food reserves into roots before shoots; it may be ten years before a moss campion produces its striking pink flowers. There are other ways to stay close to the ground, where the climate, including both temperature and wind velocity, is less severe. Some plants form small or large mats. Others creep or sprawl, often rooting from the stems as they go, tacking the plant securely to the ground.

Rounded diapensia cushion

Mat-forming alpine azalea

Rushes whipping in the wind in an alpine meadow

Hairs provide protection for some alpines. Where hairs grow on the undersides of leaves (as in Labrador tea with its tawny wool), they protect the stomata, or leaf openings, through which gases are exchanged. Several mosses in the alpine region have leaves with hair points, sometimes making them look hoary as in the gray green mats of shag moss, *Racomitrium lanuginosum,* whose specific name means "woolly."

Wind is a constant challenge for alpine plants. Narrow-leaved highland rush, deer's-hair, and Bigelow's sedge, as well as many delicate-looking alpine grasses, bend with the mountain blasts. Their buds grow at or below ground level, so they can regrow if their blades are damaged.

Alpine plants often display striking fall leaf colors—blueberries, bilberries, three-toothed cinquefoil, and alpine bearberry turn shades of bold red and purple caused by anthocyanins, the pigments found in red maple leaves and in apple skins. Many alpines have darkened leaves throughout the year. Anthocyanins absorb the higher levels of potentially damaging ultraviolet light found at these elevations.

Other aspects of alpine plant physiology are adaptive as well. Some alpines photosynthesize best at lower temperatures (55° F) than do lowland plants (70°–80° F). Alpines begin growing and absorbing nutrients at temperatures hardly above 32° F; lichens and

October leaf colors and snow above treeline

mosses do this at even lower temperatures, sometimes under a thin layer of snow. Lowland plants, however, may require temperatures of 40° F.

The spring-blooming alpines form their flower buds by the end of the previous season. Thus they are ready to bloom by early June, even in mid-May if conditions permit, and have ample late-spring and summer warmth both for seed development and food production for further growth.

What about reproductive adaptations? Alpine plants have many strategies for both successful asexual and sexual reproduction. Asexual reproduction is relatively more common in alpine plants as compared to their relatives downslope. Runners, bulblets, layering, and underground stems are all means by which alpine plants can provide their offshoots with larger amounts of food than they can provide to seeds. Three-toothed cinquefoil spreads by underground stems; some grasses and sedges form extensive turfs this way. Alpine bistort never produces seed but is "viviparous": The parent plant produces red bulblets on its stem and these fall off to form new plants. Lichens and mosses can reproduce from pieces that break off, and fir clubmoss reproduces from small, green, toothed flaps called gemmae, as well as from sexual spores. All these asexual methods produce "clones," offspring with the same genetic makeup as the parent plant.

Sexual reproduction, whether it results in seeds or spores, has the advantage of genetic recombination, which may enable a species to survive changing climatic conditions. There is much flowering and seed produc- tion above treeline, and there are a surprising number of insect pollinators. Bog and dwarf bilberries, mountain cranberries, crowberries, and blueberries produce blooms throughout the early grow- ing season. The resulting berries, so numerous and

Mountain cranberries

conspicuous in their summer and fall display, are eaten and dissemi- nated by a variety of birds and animals.

Most seeds germinate well, although some require a dormant period. The problem with sexual reproduction in the alpine zone is seedling establishment. Alpines often have fast root growth, but frost heaving and soil movement kill all but a few out of every hundred seedlings in the difficult first year. Dispersal may not be very effective in the alpine zone either; in some experiments on Franconia Ridge, three feet from the parent was a long way for a seed to travel.

The alpine areas of our northeastern mountains are sometimes called "arctic-alpine" because a large proportion of the plants are also part of the Arctic flora. This is particularly true in the Presidential Range—almost two-thirds of Mt. Washington's plants are also found in the Arctic. There are more than seven square miles of surface above timberline in the White Mountains (as com- pared with only eighty-five acres in the Adirondacks, for exam- ple)—a large area in which these plants can find their own special niches. Arctic plant communities and those above treeline in the northeastern mountains are much more similar to each other than either is to the alpine communities of western North America. Partly this is due to climatic similarities (year-round humid condi- tions instead of intense summer sun and drought) and partly due to the continuity of migration routes between the New England

mountains and the Canadian Arctic. You would see very few of
our New England alpine plants in the Rockies (or in the Alps), but
many of them live elsewhere in the circumpolar Arctic. Diapensia,
highland rush, bog bilberry, mountain cranberry, and many others
can be found in Greenland, Norway, Swedish Lapland, and Siberia.

Other plants found in the New England alpine zones, however,
are subalpine or boreal species that extend upward above treeline
into favorable habitats such as streams, ravines, or protected late-
lying snowbanks. Some, like Labrador tea, bog laurel, and small
cranberry, are bog plants at lower elevations. In the alpine zone
these plants are scaled down, have fewer shorter branches, and usually smaller leaves. They also have a speeded-up growth cycle from
the start of photosynthesis in the spring to the production of flowers
and fruit.

Alpine Plant Communities

If you are looking for particular plants, it helps to recognize the
communities in which they are found. Plants generally live in communities, often with one or two species taking up most of the room
and using most of the resources. Other less-dominant species grow
with or under them. A community is not a superorganism but a
group of plants (and usually animals, too), each of which is able to
live within a particular set of habitat factors. Communities are quite
variable. There may be a little more of one species and less of
another or an unusual species joining in as a result of changing
environmental factors or chance occurrences. Where the environment, soil type, moisture level, or wind exposure changes abruptly,
so do the communities. But more often, changes are gradual and
communities intergrade, especially the various sedge, rush, and
heath communities.

Each plant species has its own requirements and tolerances for
temperature, soil, moisture, wind speed, and late snow cover. Some
plants, like bog bilberries, are alpine generalists—members of a
number of alpine communities. But some, like alpine bluets, are at
home in a single community type only. You can become an expert
in "reading" the landscape as you watch the communities and the
environmental factors change together.

The alpine communities described below are named in terms of
their plants, as they were thirty years ago by L. C. Bliss, because the

plants are the dominant community organisms. Moreover, plants are anchored and tend to stay in place. But mobile White Mountain butterflies, various flies, spiders, and small mammals belong to these communities, too—and can be seen by careful watchers.

Diapensia Communities

Diapensia communities inhabit the windiest, most exposed sites, often ridges with little snow cover. Unlike most of the other communities, which have virtually solid plant cover, these may also include patches of bare ground. Diapensia is characterized by its attractive, compact hummock shapes. In the severest sites, diapensia no longer forms hummocks but flattens out into a mat. Little blowouts occur where part of the plant has been gouged by the wind. Alpine azalea and Lapland rosebay manage to survive with it, thus forming a community of three of the most beautiful June-flowering dwarf shrubs. Bog bilberry and highland rush are found in diapensia communities, as is the later-blooming Cutler's goldenrod. Haircap moss and several lichens, especially Iceland lichen, also grow here.

Look for these communities on Bigelow Lawn, Monroe Flats, and the summits of Mts. Eisenhower and Franklin in the White Mountains and on the Saddle on Katahdin and north of adjoining Hamlin Peak. On Franconia Ridge, both Lapland rosebay and alpine azalea are absent from the diapensia communities. They do not occur on Mt. Mansfield, and diapensia communities there are quite rare.

Diapensia community with patches of bare ground and blown-out diapensia mounds

An extensive Bigelow's sedge meadow community high on Mt. Washington

Bigelow's Sedge Meadow Communities

The most common community you will see on the upper slopes of Mt. Washington looks like a grassy field but is actually a Bigelow's sedge meadow, kept moist by frequent exposure to fog and rain. Such a meadow can be seen just below the summit on the northwest slope of Mt. Washington. Little else grows in it except mountain sandwort, which often seeds into disturbed areas along trails. Moisture-loving mosses look very green next to the tawny fall color and dark fruits of the sedge. Pure sedge meadows are absent on Franconia Ridge. They are very local on Katahdin, occurring in the vicinity of Thoreau and Caribou springs in wet, seepy soil.

Sedge/Dwarf Shrub/Heath Communities

Another community type consists of a combination of more than 50 percent Bigelow's sedge with a variety of other species. This may be called the sedge/dwarf shrub/heath community and is found on the west and north slopes of Mts. Washington, Jefferson, and Adams and also on Franconia Ridge. Mountain sandwort and mountain cranberry are its two main associates. At one Franconia Ridge site, bog bilberry and three-toothed cinquefoil are part of this community. Reindeer lichen, Iceland lichen, and haircap moss grow here. Lichens are more important in the ground cover than mosses in this community, which is less constantly moist.

Dwarf shrub/heath/rush community

Continuing down the west and north slopes of Mt. Washington, highland rush, sometimes aptly called three-forked rush, becomes a prominent plant. In some places, such as above the Great Gulf, it seems to take over huge areas, looking like a field of windblown grain. Clumps of this rush appear in the sedge/rush/dwarf shrub/heath community, a large mouthful indicating a general mixture rather than one dominant species. This community includes the turflike Bigelow's sedge, mountain cranberry, and three-toothed cinquefoil. Look also for boreal bentgrass, a sparse but attractive companion plant. Lichens often abound here, sometimes providing as much cover as each of the major vascular plant species. Highland rush/Bigelow's sedge/mountain cranberry/lichen combinations are found high up on Boott Spur and at several sites on Franconia Ridge. A similar community with conspicuous highland rush occurs on Camel's Hump in the Green Mountains.

Dwarf Shrub/Heath/Rush Communities

A very common community in the Presidential Range has much less sedge and more highland rush and dwarf shrubs. It is called the dwarf shrub/heath/rush community and covers much of the Alpine Garden, Bigelow Lawn, and is on all the other peaks usually within a few hundred feet of treeline. It is a very species-rich community—seventeen different vascular plant species as well as many mosses and lichens may be found within it. Highland rush, mountain cranberry, three-toothed cinquefoil, and bog bilberry dominate, but diapensia, Bigelow's sedge, boreal bentgrass, Cutler's goldenrod, deer's-hair sedge, and mountain sandwort are also common components. Rarer species such as Boott's rattlesnake-root can be found here, too.

On Franconia Ridge, this community contains large amounts of highland rush, mountain cranberry, reindeer lichen, Iceland lichen, and sometimes bog bilberry, as well as a significant percentage of Bigelow's sedge.

A very similar community also occurs on Mt. Mansfield and on Katahdin, where it has been called "alpine heath" by Charles Cogbill and Don Hudson, and is widespread, especially among the rock polygons on the Tableland and around Hamlin Peak. It is dominated by bog bilberry and Iceland lichen with highland rush, Bigelow's sedge, reindeer lichen, and alpine sweetgrass joining in.

Dwarf Shrub/Heath Communities

Dwarf shrub/heath communities do not have sedges or rushes as major components. Bog bilberry, mountain cranberry, Labrador tea, bunchberry, and low sweet blueberry are dominant. In the Presidentials, an average of thirteen different flowering plants are found in this community and many of these are hard to find elsewhere. Dwarf shrub/heath communities can be found near the Alpine Garden, Lakes of the Clouds, and on Mt. Monroe.

Dwarf shrub/heath community

Look for alpine sweetgrass and black crowberry, a creeping heathlike plant with black berries. Dwarf birch, a trailing tree with scallop-edged, dime-sized leaves, is found near the Lakes of the Clouds together with bog laurel, Canada mayflower, and starflower. Watch for a tiny alpine blueberry, *Vaccinium boreale,* with sharply toothed, very narrow leaves. Like other blueberries, it is handsome in its rich fall colors. Another interesting and scarce shrub on Mt. Washington and Katahdin is alpine bearberry, which has small, net-veined leaves and, in a very good summer, black berries.

The dwarf shrub/heath communities form dense mats, with crinkly brown Iceland lichen underneath the shrubs and almost no ground showing. Where there is winter snow protection, bog bilberry is the dominant species, together with Iceland lichen. Franconia Ridge has dwarf shrub/heath communities in which bog bilberry and mountain cranberry are dominant. Similar communities with bog bilberry as the dominant plant occur on Mt. Mansfield and Katahdin, often with some admixture of sedge or rush, making them hard to distinguish from the other communities described above.

Snowbank Communities

Snowbank communities occur where the snow remains late in the spring, often into July. They are the most species-rich of all the alpine communities; at least twenty-five vascular plants, as well as

Snowbank community in early June

many mosses, grow in them. Not only do these communities contain the most species, but 40 percent of the species sampled by L. C. Bliss in the Presidential Range alpine zone were found above treeline only in this type of community. Most of these species are not rare but also occur in the subalpine forests and some of them even in deciduous forests. These include Canada mayflower, goldthread, bluebead lily, bunchberry, and, most noticeably, the tall false hellebore, or Indian poke.

Dwarf bilberry is a dominant snowbank plant, as is lovely late-season hairgrass, *Deschampsia flexuosa*. The white-flowered alpine bluet is a variety restricted in New England to the White Mountain snowbank communities. This honey-scented flower is easy to find when it blooms in July. Dense snowbank communities at high elevations are also home to mountain woodfern, Bartram's shadbush, meadowsweet, twisted stalk, large-leaved goldenrod, and dwarf birches. Bigelow's sedge and bog bilberry become much more robust plants here than in their other habitats. Mosses and lichens are less prominent, but broom and feather mosses, more common in subalpine forests, occur in protected spots.

Other rare species are found where the snow lies relatively late. Two rare beauties are moss plant, *Cassiope hypnoides* (meaning like a moss), and mountain heath, *Phyllodoce*. Dwarf willow, *Salix herbacea*, is generally a plant of late-lying snow. It is common high in the

Snowbank community in early July

Great Gulf but scarce elsewhere and recently extirpated in the Adirondacks. Mountain sorrel is found in the Great Gulf. It is a common snowbank plant in the Rocky Mountains, where snowbank communities are even larger and more diverse.

Extensive snowbank communities are found on the southeast and east slopes of the upper cone of Mt. Washington adjacent to clumps of above-treeline krummholz. They can also be found in the lee of large rocks and in natural depressions. On Franconia Ridge, Charles Cogbill, who recently studied all the vegetation there quantitatively, distinguished two types of snowbank communities: heath snowbanks and herbaceous snowbanks. One Franconia Ridge site on North Lafayette is considered a heath snowbank. Labrador tea is its dominant plant, with 60 percent of the cover; two other heath shrubs, mountain cranberry and bog bilberry, are also important. Bristly clubmoss and dwarf bilberry are part of that community, as well.

Herbaceous snowbank communities on Franconia Ridge are more like those described in the Presidentials, with false hellebore, mountain woodfern, large-leaved goldenrod, bunchberry, dwarf bilberry, and mountain avens. Mountain avens is a nearly endemic species—it is found nowhere in the world except atop the White Mountains and on several small islands off the coast of Nova Scotia. A streamside as well as a snowbank plant on Mt. Washington, it is a bold accent with its large leaves and yellow flowers in midsummer, when the early profusion of spring blooms is gone.

Snowbank communities are also found on Katahdin, containing many of the same species including dwarf bilberry, bog bilberry, hairgrass, dwarf birch, moss plant, and mountain heath, as well as a variety of subalpine herbaceous plants. These communities differ from those on Mt. Washington, containing more moss plant and mountain heath and lacking mountain avens, false hellebore, and alpine bluets. Katahdin snowbank communities are found under cornices where snow builds up or at the heads of steep gullies and occasionally in depressions or on the lee side of krummholz patches. There are no true snowbank communities on Mt. Mansfield.

Streamside Communities

Streamside communities abound in the Presidentials and contain many interesting plants. More than a third of the streamside species are restricted to these sites, as are many of the mosses found in and next to the water.

Streamside community in July

Look along the trail in the Alpine Garden. Streamside community sites can be seen right from the paths and are particularly noteworthy in summer since many streamside plants bloom later than the early heaths. Silver willow, tea-leaved willow, and bearberry willow are abundant. All have conspicuous catkins, like the lowland pussy willow. Other streamside community flowers worth finding are mountain avens, harebell, alpine violet, alpine willow-herb, Boott's rattlesnake-root, and eyebright. Aquatic mosses, liverworts, and even macroscopic green algae grow right in the streams; peat, or sphagnum, moss borders them. Lichens are important in these communities, too.

Several unusual plants are found along streams and other wet areas, including painted cup, alpine bistort, spiked trisetum and mountain witchgrass, *Agropyron trachycaulon,* and the attractive hair-like sedge, *Carex capillaris.* Distinctive-looking mountain sedge, *Carex scirpoidea,* grows here, in somewhat less-moist sites. This species was once dominant on Mt. Lafayette but is now extirpated there. Two rare mosses, at home in the Arctic, occur here as well: a broom moss, *Dicranum elongatum,* and a large turgid moss resembling yellow worms, *Aulocomnium turgidum.*

On Mt. Washington, some streams are actually springs that emerge at the base of the cone and flow out across the Alpine

Garden. Alpine streamside communities are not found on Franconia Ridge, Katahdin, Mt. Mansfield, or other lower-elevation mountains in New England. Many of their distinctive species are found in New England only on Mt. Washington, so please do not disturb them.

Cotton sedge in alpine bog community on the edge of a small alpine lake

Alpine Bog Communities

Small alpine bog communities can be found south of the Lakes of the Clouds on Mt. Washington and on Mt. Mansfield. Larger bog communities exist in the Presidentials, particularly along the Crawford Path on the north side of Mt. Franklin and south of Mt. Eisenhower, as well as between Mizpah Hut and Mt. Jackson. Bogs are peat-land communities, which are fed only by rainwater and are usually very acid and low in nutrients. Bogs are underlain by sphagnum moss. Here there are several kinds, including three red species, *Sphagnum capillifolium, S. magellanicum,* and *S. rubellum,* and brown *S. fuscum.* Small, or wrens-egg, cranberries creep over the moss, and white-tufted cotton sedge is the most conspicuous plant.

Bog laurel, also found in streamside and heath snowbanks, is present in these bog communities. Cloudberry, also called "baked apple berry" for its yellow fruit, occurs in the larger bogs along the Crawford Path and in the Mahoosucs. The lovely mountain bog sedge, *Carex paupercula,* grows in small clumps on the edges of alpine bogs that surround small lakes in the alpine zone.

Birds

Many interesting birds live below treeline in the spruce-fir and balsam fir zones. Do not miss the chance to do some bird-watching (and listening) on your way up the mountain.

There are birds to be found on the summits as well. Gray jays will greet you, and probably steal your sandwiches, too, on Mt. Jackson and other peaks. Crows are not generally found at these elevations, but acrobatic ravens will soar, tumble, and give their coarse croaking call. Ravens nest on Mt. Mansfield on the cliffs northeast of the Chin. Juncos with their round forms and conspicuous white tail feathers commonly nest in the alpine zone. Their song is a continuous trill that sounds like a musical sewing machine. Also breeding in the alpine zone are white-throated sparrows. The male has brighter white stripes and a yellow spot near the eye in breeding plumage. He may seek you out and answer your whistle if you imitate his clear "Old Sam Peabody Peabody."

Black-and-white-striped blackpolls and yellow-rumped warblers are sometimes found above treeline, though they usually nest in the subalpine forest trees. A pair of yellow-rumped warblers was found nesting in one of the small bogs on Mt. Mansfield. Bicknell's thrushes are seen regularly in the alpine zone on Mt. Mansfield and nest in the subalpine forest as do boreal chickadees and golden-crowned kinglets. These birds are found in the Presidentials and on Katahdin as well.

American pipits, brown birds with long legs and white tail feathers, can be seen on all the New England alpine summits, especially in the fall during their migration south from breeding grounds in the Arctic tundra. They spend the winter flocking in fields and beaches from southern New England southward. Some also nest on mountaintops in the Rockies and also on Katahdin. They have recently been seen courting and nesting on Mt. Washington and are currently under study by the New Hampshire Audubon Society. If you see a pipit there in the summer, be sure to report it to the AMC at Pinkham Notch.

Birds in the Alpine Zone

Common raven
Corvus corax

Unmistakable raucous black bird; 24"; heavy bill; wedge-shaped tail; shaggy throat feathers; distinctive croak; watch for aerial acrobatics; in alpine and lower zones

Dark-eyed junco
Junco hyemalis

Sings and breeds on all New England summits; 6"; slate gray, round bird with white belly; white outer tail feathers; trilling song, like a musical sewing machine

American pipit
Anthus rubescens

Brown-streaked ground bird; slender bill; 6-7"; white tail feathers; pumps tail up and down as it walks; fall visitor to New England summits; breeds on Katahdin

Boreal chickadee

Parus hudsonicus

Similar to black-capped chickadee but with a brown cap and slower, more nasal call; 5"; breeds in sub-alpine forests and north to Hudson Bay and Alaska

White-throated sparrow

Zonotrichia albicollis

White throat; distinctive black-and-white crown; breeding male has yellow "eyebrow"; 7"; breeds in all New England alpine areas; whistles "Old Sam Peabody"

Gray jay or Canada jay

Perisoreus canadensis

Gray-backed, white below; 12"; juveniles are sooty; widespread in N. America; New England sub-species has white forehead, brownish crown; not shy

Black-backed woodpecker

Picoides arcticus

Two yellow-capped woodpeckers are found in New England sub-alpine forests; the rarer three-toed woodpecker, *P. tridactylus,* has a barred back; 12"

Bill Silliker, Jr.

Spruce grouse

Dendragapus canadensis

Brown, chickenlike ground bird;
perches in trees; 16"; male has
dark throat, red eye comb; found
in spruce-fir and fir forests; tamer
than ruffed grouse

Blackpoll warbler

Dendroica striata

Streaked with black and white,
black cap, white cheeks; 5"; sings
a high *zi, zi, zi*; nests in conifers
near treeline; breeds n. to Alaska;
winters in S. America;

B. Henry/VIREO

Red crossbill

Loxia curvirostra

This bird and white-winged crossbill, *L. leucoptera,* 6½"; have
unique crossed bill tips used to
extract conifer seeds; females are
drab olive, males are brick red

Golden-crowned kinglet

Regulus satrapa

Tiny round bird; 4"; common up
to treeline; easily heard but hard
to see; along with ruby-crowned
kinglet, breeds in lower-elevation
conifer forests in New England

Magnolia warbler

Dendroica magnolia

Usually found in conifer forests, sometimes to treeline; yellow breast with dark streaks; 5"; clear whistled song; winters in Caribbean and Central America

Yellow-rumped warbler

Dendroica coronata

Warbler most likely to be seen in the alpine zone; yellow throat, side, cap, and rump; 5"; slender; narrow bill; an insect eater; lines nest with many feathers

Bicknell's thrush

Catharus bicknelli

Very similar to gray-cheeked thrush but with browner back, different song; 8"; breeds in New England subalpine forests; related to Swainson's and hermit thrushes

Winter wren

Troglodytes troglodytes

Tiny 4" bird with stubby cocked tail; very long, beautiful song; sometimes seen at treeline; nests in conifer forests north and west to Alaska, winters in s. U.S.

Amphibians

None of the amphibians or
reptiles that inhabit the New
England mountains are truly
alpine or alpine-arctic. This
is in strong contrast to the
large alpine flora but is not
surprising in view of the
challenging climatic conditions.

Red-spotted newt (eft stage),
Notophthalmus viridescens

Ectothermic, or cold-
blooded, vertebrates, which
cannot sustain a high internal
temperature, are not well
adapted for extreme cold.
Fish, snakes, lizards, and tur-
tles are all absent from the
alpine zone. Brook trout and
slimy sculpins are found in
mountain streams but not
very high up. Reptiles do
not make it far up either.
The red-bellied snake is an
occasional visitor near bogs
at medium elevations, and
there may be a turtle in a
medium-elevation pond.

American toad, *Bufo americanus*

Amphibians are another
matter. Red efts (the land
stage of aquatic red-spotted
newts), American toads, and
spring peepers are often seen
quite high up on the trails;
the latter inhabit Eagle Lakes
east of Greenleaf Hut. Mink
frogs probably breed in the
mountains, too. Dusky,
red-backed, and two-lined
salamanders are reportedly
found at medium elevations

Wood frog, *Rana sylvatica*

Mink frog, *Rana septentrionalis*

in the White Mountains. Dusky and two-lined salamanders and red-spotted newts lay their eggs in the water and have an aquatic swimming larval stage. The red-backed salamander, however, has a very unusual life cycle. It lays its eggs on land, and bypasses the aquatic larval stage altogether. The female guards the eggs until they hatch into tiny salamanders.

Hikers have reported seeing frogs at 5,200 feet on Mt. Washington in one of the Lakes of the Clouds, which are shallow and freeze solid in the winter. They may be mink frogs, wood frogs, or toads laying their eggs. This mystery remains to be solved.

Mammals

Mammals are relatively rare on the New England alpine summits. Some species, however, are easily seen on your way up the mountains. Red squirrels are at home in the spruce-fir and fir forests. They are active during the day, throughout the year, and eat a variety of fruits, nuts, conifer seeds, eggs, and fungi, which they store in crotches of trees. The red squirrel is thus part of many food chains and is itself eaten by martens and other predators.

Moose can also be seen on your climbs, particularly on Katahdin.

Bull moose, *Alces alces*

There the moose, including cows with calves, tend to stay around ponds and wet-lands in the summer, eating aquatic vegetation. In the fall, they move up the mountain and browse in or near the krummholz, even high up on the Appalachian Trail, browsing on twigs, bark, and perhaps lichens. Moose occasionally traverse the White Mountain sum-mits as well. They are big, powerful animals. Moose may look awkward but can swim as fast as two people can paddle a canoe and can

Snowshoe hare, *Lepus americanus*

run up to 35 MPH on land. Beware of moose on the highway at night; in New Hampshire and Maine, motorists on the mountain roads are more likely to be killed by moose than by drunk drivers.

Two mammals that you are very likely to see above treeline are snowshoe hares and, high on Mt. Washington, woodchucks! Woodchucks belong to the same genus as the whistling marmots of the western mountains, but we don't usually think of them far from vegetable gardens. Like snowshoe hares, they have a wide range, from Hudson Bay in the East to Alaska in the West. Woodchucks are actually beneficial outside of agricultural areas since they dig burrows that later become homes for other furbearers. They are largely diurnal animals and eat a variety of plants. They hibernate for about five months of the year, but you may see them feeding or hear them whistle near their burrows on a warm sunny day on Mt. Washington.

Snowshoe hares are commonly found on all the New England mountains, as evidenced by their scat. They are comparable in size to eastern cottontails, which do not occur on New England moun-tains. Snowshoe hares sometimes defend territories during the breeding season but at other times may wander up to one mile. There are many dangers in a snowshoe hare's life, especially in the alpine zone, and they rarely live longer than three years in the wild. Snowshoe hares are dark brown in summer and turn camouflage

Marten, *Martes americana*

white in winter, the key to their second common name: varying hare. Look for their tracks. Their big feet act rather like snowshoes for snowy winter travel. Unlike woodchucks, snowshoe hares are largely nocturnal and may hide under brush or krummholz trees during the day. In winter, snowshoe hares must survive on twigs, bark, and buds. In summer, they feed on a variety of vegetation. In addition to their other challenges, the "amazing alpine plants" must cope with hungry herbivores!

Other, rarely seen animals have been sighted or trapped in the alpine zone. Bobcats and lynx are visitors there, as are members of the carnivorous weasel family. Short-tailed weasels, like snowshoe hares, turn pure white in winter. Long-tailed weasels prey on shrews and voles. Martens, also members of the weasel family, are sometimes seen quite high up. Martens live in northern regions of New York and New England and in Canada. They are also found along the Pacific coast, in the Rocky Mountains, and in Alaska. Their yellowish brown fur is distinctive. Martens spend much of their time in trees but also forage on the ground. They are largely carnivorous, feeding on red squirrels and other small animals as well as birds, insects, and even fruits and nuts. They den in trees or logs but may range as far as fifteen miles, traveling at least occasionally into the alpine zone. Martens and their larger relatives, fishers, have both been observed along the trails up Katahdin. Fishers have dark brown coats with white-tipped hairs. They were once more common in our mountain forests but were nearly trapped out for their beautiful fur. Like martens, they are also mainly carnivorous and are one of the few predators that feed on porcupines.

Carnivorous shrews must catch and eat food equivalent to their own weight every day, year-round. It is hard to see how they can survive on our mountain summits, but several species have been trapped above timberline. These include smoky shrews and short-tailed shrews, which have poisonous saliva used to paralyze prey. Pygmy shrews of mountain slope forests are probably the smallest living mammals, each weighing no more than a dime. Pygmy shrews have been found on Mt. Mansfield; their habits await further study. The rare long-tailed shrew has been trapped in Tuckerman Ravine.

Various types of mice, lemmings, and voles also live in the Mt. Washington area, on Katahdin, and on the other New England summits. These rodents are herbivores and feed on whatever sort of vegetable food they can find, including sedges, grasses, seeds, and berries of high-elevation plants. Mice have large ears and eyes and long tails. Lemmings and voles have smaller ears and eyes, short tails, and usually longer fur. You can find some member of this family (which also includes rats and muskrats) wherever you are in North America. Common lowland species such as meadow voles and white-footed mice get pretty high up the mountains; the latter is likely to enter buildings. Brownish gray northern bog lemmings are active day and night and live in subalpine and alpine meadows in northern New England, Canada, and Alaska. They are rare in our mountains, so if you see a four-inch, rounded, mouselike creature with concealed ears and a short tail in the sedge meadows, you have made a rare discovery. Yellow-nose voles also inhabit alpine meadows. They have a similar shape, size, and color but with bright yellow noses and longer tails.

Insects

Insects above treeline are intriguing subjects. How do they manage with the weather conditions there? They wait for the sun to give them sufficient body heat. On sunny days in July, you can see numerous White Mountain butterflies mating in the Alpine Garden. Thus distracted, they can be easily photographed. Solitary individuals shoot up from their resting places as you approach and sail quickly off with the wind. As striped caterpillars, they feed on Bigelow's sedge. White Mountain butterflies are an endemic variety, *Oeneis melissa semidea,* found nowhere else in the world. Relatives in the same genus live in alpine and arctic regions in much of the world, including the Rocky Mountains and the Alps. Half a dozen different kinds of butterfly flit across the summer alpine landscape, searching out flowers on those rare sunny and

White Mountain butterflies, *Oeneis melissa semidea*

calm days. Among them are orange-and-black fritillaries, of which there is an endemic variety on Mt. Washington.

The other New England mountain summits have their share of insects, too. Tiger swallowtails and monarch butterflies can be seen on high ridges. Katahdin has its own endemic species, *Oeneis polixenes katahdin,* the Katahdin Arctic butterfly. This small, mottled butterfly is well camouflaged among the alpine rocks and lichens.

A number of alpine plants are pollinated by butterflies. Moss campion's pink flowers have narrow nectar-holding tubes and can only be pollinated by these long-tongued insects. Other plants, like Labrador tea, are pollinated by solitary bumblebees. Most flowers in the alpine zone are pollinated by flies, of which there is a large variety. Early season, tiny, biting blackflies are the scourge of humans in the mountains. Later there are nonbiting bee flies, which mimic stinging striped bees but have two wings, not four.

In late August on Mt. Washington, White Mountain butterflies are no longer in evidence, but green-and-black-striped alpine grasshoppers, *Booneacris glacialis,* mate on the rocks. Wolf spiders, common throughout the summer, are busy hunting their prey. Their dark color helps them absorb precious solar heat. Butterfly and moth caterpillars feed on alpine plants. Great and Saint Lawrence tiger moths have large, multicolored "woolly bear" caterpillars. Both are arctic species that overwinter on the summits as caterpillars. The southern limit to their range is the alpine summits

Great tiger moth caterpillar, *Arctia caja*

Saint Lawrence tiger moth caterpillar,
Platarctia parthenos

Black wolf spider of the family Lycosidae

Alpine booney grasshoppers, *Booneacris
glacialis*

of the northeastern U.S.

Little has been written for the public on alpine insects, much less those of the New England summits, but Ann Zwinger and Beatrice Willard discuss insect pollinators in their book *Land Above the Trees*. The museum in the Mt. Washington summit building has an insect exhibit. It tells about the muscid fly, *Phaonia rugia*, which is only found at and above treeline and feeds on the pollen of mountain avens. The adult life of the fly coincides with the flowering of this plant. The larva of a wingless scorpion fly, *Boreus brumalis,* is reported to feed on mosses.

Entomologists swarmed to Mt. Washington in the nineteenth century. Samuel Scudder reported twenty-two different species of butterflies on the highest summits. One of the earliest and most proficient women entomologists to explore the White Mountains was Annie T. Slosson, who recorded five hundred different species of flies in the Mt. Washington alpine zone in the 1890s.

More information is needed. Watch the alpine pollinators and other insect and spider life on a warm sunny day and see what you can discover.

Conservation of our rare and interesting alpine flora and fauna should be the concern of all who enjoy the New England mountains. There are many ways in which we can help—or at least prevent future harm—to the very special alpine ecosystems.

Conservation of the rare plants of the White Mountains has been a major concern of the AMC and other government and private agencies at least since the 1930s. At that time S. K. Harris and Fred Steele warned against the mass collecting of rare plants that had occurred over the past one hundred years. Plants weren't the only victims. Annie T. Slosson wrote in 1895 about the beetle collectors: "The summit looked as if shaken by an earthquake, the ground was full of holes and pits of irregular shapes, from which heavy stones had been dragged by the . . . eager collectors; . . . alpine beetles were in serious danger of extinction."

The rules for protecting alpine species are simple. Do not pick any flowers or collect any creatures on these mountaintops. Stay on the trails and within designated areas near the huts. Do not take rock samples; doing so can disturb the special habitats of both plants and animals.

The high peaks of the Green Mountains in Vermont and the Adirondacks in New York, with relatively small alpine zones, have summit stewards on duty during the warmer months. Their mission is to educate climbers about the alpine flora and fauna and urge them to stay on the trails. A child on the top of Mt. Mansfield was recently heard calling to her father, "Don't step there! It's not grass; it's rare plants"—a message from a summit steward. In Baxter State Park, with its numerous trailheads, and in the White Mountains, with more extensive alpine zones, summit stewards are less feasible. Katahdin has an excellent conservation education program and in the White Mountains, well-dramatized conservation messages are given daily by AMC hut personnel.

Some species in the alpine zone are very rare, or even endemic, occurring nowhere else in the world. Dwarf cinquefoil, *Potentilla robbinsiana,* lives only in the White Mountains. It was first collected on Monroe Flats in 1824, and since that time more than eight hundred specimens of this threatened plant have been removed by botanists. In spite of overcollecting and heavy Crawford Path traffic essentially right over this population, dwarf cinquefoil still survives at this site, but it is on the federal Endangered Species List. The

CONSERVATION

Dwarf cinquefoil conservation area protected by a low scree wall

AMC, together with the U.S. Forest Service, has developed strategies to protect the dwarf cinquefoil in its special habitat. In 1984, the Crawford Path was relocated and a low scree wall built around the dwarf cinquefoil site. You are not allowed to enter this area. A recent study of the dwarf cinquefoil population by Melissa Iszard-Crowley is encouraging: The population itself has increased greatly over the past eight years. In particular, the number of plants that produced flowers and seeds increased by 60 percent between 1984 and 1992. These plants often do not bloom until they are twenty years old but then have a long life span. Because of the success of the recovery plan, the dwarf cinquefoil may come off the endangered list—but only if all of us take care to see that its habitat continues to be protected.

Human activities have caused major changes and the local extinction of several alpine plants species on Franconia Ridge. Other very rare species have been eliminated from their former mountaintop sites but still occur in relatively inaccessible locations. Many groups have carried out restoration projects on Franconia Ridge. Begun in 1977, the technique that seems to have worked best is the construction of low scree walls bordering both sides of the ridge trail. These have defined the trail, stopped the off-trail trampling by hikers' boots, and allowed the vegetation to recover naturally. Rock cairns, paint marks, and educational signs also help to keep

AMC hut crew packs out trash from Lakes Hut to Mt. Washington summit

hikers on the trail. Questionnaire results show that for a very high percentage of hikers, these techniques are both effective and unobtrusive.

Scree walls are an innovative method for both controlling hiker disturbance of alpine vegetation and preserving the backcountry experience. A somewhat unexpected, but logical, outcome is that the scree walls themselves create a sheltered microhabitat that encourage the reestablishment of alpine vegetation. These walls are costly to construct but allow passive management over a long period with very minimal taxpayer expense.

Future vigilance is needed to protect all the wild inhabitants of our New England alpine zones. You can help. Stay on the trails. Walk on rock wherever possible. Learn about the fascinating and often beautiful plants and animals of this fragile alpine environment. Teach others what you have learned so that they can become caring stewards as well.

$\mathcal{S}$ELECTED REFERENCES

🍃 Bliss, Lawrence C. *Alpine Zone of the Presidential Range.* 1963. Reprint. Boston: Appalachian Moutain Club. 🍃 Marchand, Peter J. *North Woods: An Inside Look at the Nature of Forests in the Northeast.* Boston: Appalachian Moutain Club, 1987. 🍃 Steele, Frederic L. *At Timberline, A Nature Guide to the Mountains of the Northeast.* Boston: Appalachian Mountain Club, 1982. 🍃 Vitt, D. H., J. E. Marsh, and R. B. Bovey. *Mosses, Lichens and Ferns of Northeast North America.* Edmundton: Lone Pine Publishing, 1988. 🍃 Waterman, Laura, and Guy Waterman. *Forest and Crag: A History of Hiking, Trail Blazing and Adventure in the Northeast Mountains.* Boston: Appalachian Mountain Club, 1989. 🍃 Zwinger, Ann H., and Beatrice Willard. *Land Above the Trees, A Guide to American Alpine Tundra.* New York: Harper and Row, 1972. Reprint. University of Arizona Press, 1989.

🍃 Scientific names of vascular plants follow Gleason, H. A., and A. C. Cronquist. *Manual of Vascular Plants of the Northeastern United States and Adjacent Canada.* 2d ed. New York: New York Botanical Garden, 1991.